Book 6

Keys to Good Language

A Comprehensive Program
for Language Skills
with a
Complete "Keyed" Handbook

Phoenix Learning Resources, LLC.

Phoenix Learning Resources, LLC.

910 Church Street • Honesdale, PA 18431
1-800-228-9345 • Fax: 570-253-3227 • www.phoenixlearningresources.com

Item# 1175   ISBN 978-0-7915-1175-6

Contents

Contents

The Text begins on page 52.

Effective Sentences
                                                                    ⊙━ 44

An effective sentence expresses a thought clearly. An ineffective sentence leaves the reader in doubt about what is being said.

I.   Check the more effective sentence in each pair below. (Score: 20)

_____ 1.   Getting to the bus stop, the bus was there.

_____   When I got to the bus stop, the bus was there.

_____ 2.   The boy lived next door to me who moved yesterday.

_____   The boy who lived next door to me moved yesterday.

_____ 3.   Trish got angry when I slammed the door.

_____   I slammed the door, which Trish got angry.

_____ 4.   It's fun to swing from limb to limb in the big trees.

_____   Where the trees are big enough it's fun to swing from limb to limb.

_____ 5.   We are held on earth by the laws of gravity.

_____   We are held on earth by the force of gravity.

_____ 6.   English is when you speak good.

_____   English is the language we speak.

_____ 7.   Does an impala run faster than a race horse?

_____   Is the speed of an impala greater than a race horse?

_____ 8.   She likes to write all kinds of reports, such as science.

_____   She likes to write reports on such subjects as science.

_____ 9.   Capillary action takes place when a blotter soaks up ink.

_____   Capillary action is a blotter soaking up ink.

_____ 10.   I remember the humor in *Homer Price.*

_____   When I think of *Homer Price,* it is the humor.

II. Rewrite the sentences below to make them clear and effective. (Score: 20)

11.   Rounding second base, the ball was dropped. _____

_____

12.   I won the race, which my friends were pleased. _____

_____

13.   Is the height of the Ross Building more than Grogan's Hill. _____

_____

14.   When she thinks of the mountains, it is the pine trees. _____

_____

Kinds of Sentences   🗝 6 a, 7 a, 8 a, 44 b, c, d

A *declarative* sentence tells something or makes a statement. It is followed by a period.

An *interrogative sentence* asks a question. It is followed by a question mark.

An *exclamatory sentence* expresses surprise, sudden joy, sorrow, pain, fear, or excitement. It is followed by an exclamation point.

Examples: Tony visited his aunt in Florida.   _____ *declar.*

Have you ever been to Florida?   _____ *interrog.*

What a beautiful state Florida is!   _____ *exclam.*

Fill each blank with the abbreviation for the kind of sentence at the left. Place the correct punctuation mark at the end of each sentence. (Score: 2 for each sentence)

Sponges

1.   Are sponges plants or animals   _____

2.   What unusual animals they are   _____

3.   They grow on the bottom of the ocean   _____

4.   Some sponges grow 1.5 meters (5 feet) tall   _____

5.   Are all sponges brown and yellow   _____

6.   How brightly colored living sponges are   _____

7.   Sponge divers ride in unusual boats   _____

8.   Is the bottom of the boat made of glass   _____

9.   Often a sponge diver pours oil on the water   _____

10.   How clear and still the water becomes   _____

11.   The diver can see sponges 15 meters (50 feet) below   _____

12.   Does the diver hook sponges with a long pole   _____

13.   Did this sponge come from Florida   _____

14.   It came from Tarpon Springs, Florida   _____

15.   Is it a sheep's-wool sponge   _____

16.   Rita has a large sheep's-wool sponge   _____

The Complete Subject

45 a, f

The *complete subject* is the word or group of words that tells what the sentence is about. It tells the person, the place, or the thing about which something is said.

In the sentences below draw a line under the complete subjects.

Example: The ocean is the home of many animals.

Three Sea Animals

1. The largest animal on earth lives in the ocean.
2. Most whales live in groups, or schools.
3. These animals have a keen sense of hearing.
4. A thick layer of fat keeps whales warm in cold water.
5. A whale holds its breath under water.
6. The air in its lungs becomes hot and full of moisture.
7. The whale blows out its breath above the surface of the water.
8. The marine turtle is a unique inhabitant of the sea.
9. A turtle's hard upper shell is constructed of about 50 bones.

10. Turtles live much longer than most other animals.
11. An adult turtle's average age is 30 to 50 years.
12. These reptiles eat both plant and animal matter.
13. Some turtles hibernate during the coldest periods of the year.
14. The turtle's appearance has remained the same for about 200 million years.
15. The octopus's snakelike arms have suction cups on their bottom sides.
16. These allow the octopus to grab and hold anything nearby.
17. These unusual animals catch fish and crabs for food.
18. They usually try to escape from anything larger than small sea animals.
19. A swift stream of water is spurted out of the octopus's body.
20. The force of the water pushes the animal rapidly backward.
21. The octopus's color may be changed to match its surroundings.
22. Its coloring may turn from brown to red, blue, yellow, or green.
23. A cloud of black ink can be thrown out by the frightened animal.
24. A cornered octopus may use its long arms to entangle the intruding enemy.

Other Things to Do: Write two declarative, two exclamatory, and two interrogative sentences about another unusual animal.

The Complete Predicate

⊶ 45 a, g

The *complete predicate* is the word or group of words that tells something about the subject.

Draw one line under the complete predicate in each sentence below. (Score: 1 for each sentence)

Example: Tourists visit Mexico each year.

A Market Place in Mexico

1. Large supermarkets are found in the modern cities of Mexico.

2. They are able to serve many people in the busy cities.

3. Small villages may have their own market place.

4. A village might be built around a square, or plaza.

5. Modern buildings may surround the square.

6. A towering cathedral may stand on one side of the square.

7. A colorful scene is spread across the plaza in front of the cathedral.

8. The busy market place is there.

9. Rows of stalls display colorful goods for sale.

10. Farm products are also displayed at the market place.

11. People come throughout the day to buy from the vendors.

12. The vendor in that stall is selling beautiful pottery.

13. The potters dug their clay from the ground.

14. The clay was shaped on a whirling potter's wheel.

15. Village artists made their own designs for the pottery.

16. No two pieces of the pottery are alike.

17. The silver jewelry in this stall was made by hand.

18. Some of the jewelry makers have put brightly colored stones in rings and bracelets.

19. A large fountain is at one end of the plaza.

20. Flowers are sold at this end of the market place.

21. Various food stands tempt hungry shoppers.

22. Each food vendor sells something different and delicious.

23. The basketmakers offer baskets of every size and shape.

24. Some baskets are filled with straw flowers.

25. The people gather their unsold goods at the end of the day.

26. The goods may later be sold in large cities.

The Complete Sentence

Every sentence has a subject and a predicate.

Combine the groups of words in the first column with the groups of words in the second column to make complete sentences. Write the sentences on the lines below. Punctuate each sentence correctly. (Score: 3 for each sentence)

1.	An orchestra	leads the orchestra
2.	Each musician	is an important instrument
3.	Usually the conductor	are wind instruments
4.	The violin	have their own orchestras
5.	The clarinet and French horn	is made up of many musicians
6.	Most large cities	are given in parks and schools
7.	Concerts	plays an instrument

1. _____

_____

2. _____

_____

3. _____

_____

4. _____

_____

5. _____

_____

6. _____

_____

7. _____

_____

Recognizing Sentences

A *sentence* is a group of words that expresses a complete thought.

Write *Yes* at the left of each group of words that is a sentence. Write *No* at the left of each group that is not a sentence.

Examples: _____*Yes*_____ Joanie brought some interesting rocks to show us

_____*No*_____ Rocks that she picked up along the coast of Oregon

Some Interesting Rocks

_____ 1. Like to collect and study rocks

_____ 2. Last summer in Arkansas I found a piece of hard, black rock

_____ 3. The rock picked up needles and pins

_____ 4. A rock very much like a magnet

_____ 5. The first compass needles were made from rocks like this

_____ 6. Aren't these rocks sometimes called loadstones

_____ 7. A flint arrowhead from the county museum

_____ 8. Will the flint scratch glass

_____ 9. Making a spark with a piece of flint and a piece of steel

_____ 10. People used to start their fires with steel and flint

_____ 11. Tiny seashells in this piece of limestone

_____ 12. Lived millions of years ago

_____ 13. Their shells were preserved in the limestone

_____ 14. An ancient leaf in this sandstone rock

_____ 15. Plants and animals preserved in rocks are called fossils

_____ 16. This piece of lava came from Oregon

_____ 17. Long ago the lava flowed from a great volcano

_____ 18. Hardened into rock as it cooled

_____ 19. These beautiful agates came from Oregon, too

_____ 20. Wish to find some other kinds of rocks next summer

The Simple Subject

45 b

The *simple subject* is the word that names the person, the place, or the thing about which something is said.

Draw a line under the simple subject in each sentence below.

Examples: He likes to read stories about horses.

The new library is a very interesting place.

About Libraries and Books

1.   Today I went to the new library for the first time.
2.   We have learned to use the card catalogue.
3.   You may get your books from the stack by yourself.
4.   Colorful book jackets are displayed on the bulletin board.
5.   Every library is a treasury of information and adventure.
6.   Bob is trying to find exciting tales about famous Americans.
7.   Yesterday he checked out a book about Susan B. Anthony.
8.   Science books appeal to Tanya's interest in biology.
9.   Have you read any books about the human brain?
10.   My sisters enjoyed reading *Shirley Chisolm: A Biography.*
11.   Now they would like to read other stories about people in American government.
12.   Your brother will laugh at every page of *The Future of Hooper Toote.*
13.   Humorous stories are fun to read.
14.   An exciting adventure story is sure to attract the attention of Carlos and Jenny.
15.   They have just read *Call It Courage*, by Armstrong Sperry.
16.   It tells about a Polynesian boy's battle with fear of the sea.
17.   Do the dark blue illustrations show the boy's struggles?
18.   Many show the island setting of the story.
19.   Have you read *Wanted: A Horse!*
20.   It is a story about a Norwegian boy and his horse.
21.   Everyone enjoys the amusing story *Honk: The Moose.*
22.   Cold weather forced the moose to seek shelter in a barn.
23.   What funny things happened after that!
24.   Those students have formed a library club.
25.   These members have designed the club's membership buttons.
26.   Several have read four books since the beginning of school.

Other Things to Do: Write five sentences about books you have enjoyed. Draw a line under the simple subject in each of your sentences.

The Simple Predicate

The *simple predicate* is the single word or group of words that expresses action or being about the subject.

Draw a line under the simple predicate in each of the following sentences.

Example: The children <u>had</u> <u>been</u> <u>talking</u> about famous people.

Courageous Americans

1. Courageous Americans worked for the development of our civilization.

2. Many of these people concerned themselves with social problems.

3. Even in the face of ridicule, they fought for a better world.

4. You have heard about Clara Barton's work.

5. During the Civil War, she helped injured soldiers on the battlefield.

6. Later she founded the American Red Cross.

7. Abraham Lincoln was another great American.

8. As President, he influenced the course of world history.

9. Mr. Lincoln is remembered as an inspiring speaker.

10. He delivered his famous Gettysburg Address in 1863.

11. Martin Luther King, Jr., crusaded for human rights.

12. In 1964 Dr. King was awarded the Nobel Peace Prize.

13. At one time no women in our country were allowed to vote.

14. The importance of women's views in government was stressed by Susan B. Anthony.

15. Tirelessly she had crusaded for woman suffrage.

16. At last the fight was won.

17. As a child Jane Addams worried about the hardships of mill workers.

18. As an adult she established a neighborhood center for less fortunate people.

19. They went to the center for food, clothing, recreation, and medical care.

20. Jane Addams will be remembered for her charity work at Hull House.

21. Other people have devoted their time and energy to science or art.

22. Amelia Earhart is famous for her role in the development of aviation.

23. She was the first woman to fly across the Atlantic Ocean.

24. Later, she flew from California to Honolulu successfully.

25. Albert Einstein was a brilliant American scientist.

26. He is known for his theory of relativity.

27. This theory contributed to modern science.

28. What other contributions to our culture have been made by Americans of courage?

Kinds of Nouns

Words that name persons, places, or things are called *nouns.* **Common** *nouns* **are general nouns.** *Proper nouns* **are the names of particular persons, places, or things.**

In the sentences below draw one line under each common noun and two lines under each proper noun.

Example: Mr. Moore visited the museum on the Fourth of July.

A Glimpse of London

1.   The British Isles are two large islands off the coast of Europe.

2.   England is in the southern part of the British Isles.

3.   It is separated from France by a narrow body of water called the English Channel.

4.   This channel connects the Atlantic Ocean and the North Sea.

5.   Many ships sail up the Thames River from the sea to London.

6.   London Bridge used to span the broad Thames.

7.   Ms. Lewis said that she sang a song about that bridge when she was young.

8.   Near the former location of the bridge is a group of very old buildings.

9.   A shallow ditch and a high wall run around these buildings.

10.   This group of buildings is called the Tower of London.

11.   Once it was used as a fortress, a home for the king, and a jail.

12.   Today it is a museum where British treasures are displayed.

13.   Guards wear colorful costumes like those worn centuries ago.

14.   From a tall building you can see great distances in the city.

15.   New skyscrapers have been built in this city.

16.   Here and there spires of churches point to the sky.

17.   Westminster Abbey is a beautiful old church with twin towers.

18.   For a thousand years English kings and queens have been crowned there.

19.   The center of the city is crowded with traffic.

20.   One can see bicycles and cars traveling on the left side of the street.

21.   The busiest spot in London is Piccadilly Circus.

22.   This is a great, round, open space where several streets come together.

23.   The people of this busy city enjoy visiting peaceful parks.

24.   In Hyde Park they like to watch the graceful swans.

Singular and Plural Nouns

If the word in parentheses is singular, fill the blank with its plural form. If the word is plural, fill the blank with its singular form.

Examples: (patch)   Your hands carry _____*patches*_____ of living creatures.

(microscopes)   These germs may be seen through a _____*microscope*_____ .

Discovery of an Unseen World

1. (discovery)   You would make many _____ exploring a new world.

2. (plant)   What unusual _____ and animals you might find!

3. (worlds)   Three hundred years ago a Dutch naturalist found a new _____ .

4. (eye)   It was a world that had never been seen by human _____ .

5. (journey)   Anton van Leeuwenhoek didn't make _____ to other planets.

6. (lens)   He ground _____ that made small things look larger.

7. (glass)   These small _____ were the first microscopes.

8. (object)   Through them Leeuwenhoek observed many small _____ .

9. (tooth)   He saw living things in scrapings from his _____ .

10. (ponds)   What odd plants and animals he saw in water from a _____ !

11. (deer)   Did some animals look like the antlers of _____ ?

12. (fish)   They looked like _____ in a tiny sea.

13. (leaf)   The plants did not have _____ .

14. (arteries)   Leeuwenhoek took blood from a small _____ in his body.

15. (body)   He described the tiny _____ , or cells, making up the blood.

16. (life)   Leeuwenhoek didn't know that his work would affect our _____ .

17. (key)   He gave scientists _____ to understanding causes of diseases.

18. (day)   Since the _____ of Leeuwenhoek, we have learned more about germs.

Other Things to Do: Write five sentences, using the plurals of the following nouns:
cherry, mouse, knife, half, box.

Common Abbreviations

Use a period after an abbreviation.

Write the abbreviation of each of the following words.

Examples:

Monday   *Mon.*   Texas   *Tex.*

1. Thursday		21. Road
2. Tuesday		22. Company
3. Wednesday		23. Building
4. Sunday		24. Mister
5. Saturday		25. Mistress
6. Friday		26. Doctor
7. December		27. Reverend
8. January		28. Colonel
9. April		29. Oklahoma
10. August		30. California
11. November		31. Arizona
12. February		32. Mississippi
13. October		33. Kentucky
14. March		34. Tennessee
15. September		35. New York
16. North		36. Nebraska
17. Southwest		37. Oregon
18. Street		38. Colorado
19. Avenue		39. South Carolina
20. Boulevard		40. New Jersey

Other Things to Do: Write the abbreviations for *District of Columbia* and *United States of America.*

Capitalization

In the sentences below draw a line under each word that should begin with a capital letter.

Example: last friday david brought a swiss music box to school.

Switzerland, Land of Mountains

1. Last monday bill barnes and i were looking at a map of the world.
2. bill put his finger on a small yellow spot in the middle of europe.
3. ''this little country is surrounded by france, germany, and italy,'' he said.
4. the state of new york is about three times as large as that country.
5. bill said, ''we know someone who visited that place last june.''
6. we asked mrs. roberti to tell us about her trip to switzerland.
7. it is a country of mountains, glaciers, waterfalls, and lakes.
8. ''aren't the alps the highest mountains in switzerland?'' Sheila asked.
9. one of the most famous peaks is the matterhorn.
10. mountain climbers come all the way from america to scale its formidable heights.
11. in the alps the rhine river starts its long journey to the north sea.
12. look at these pictures of the blue water in crescent-shaped lake geneva.
13. here are photographs of chalets, the mountain homes of the swiss.
14. there are stone retaining walls built on farms along the sides of mountains.
15. these walls keep landslides from burying the farm buildings.
16. During the winter holidays many europeans come to the alps to ski.
17. it is bitterly cold in the mountainous regions of switzerland.
18. But winds from the mediterranean sea warm the southern fringe of the country.
19. the name of the capital, Berne, comes from a german word that means ''bears.''
20. wooden or metal statues of bears may be seen in all parts of berne.
21. the swiss children like to visit the bear pits along the banks of the aar river.
22. on market street in berne there is a very old clock that most tourists enjoy.
23. There is no swiss language, so most of the people speak french, german, or italian.
24. mr. j. h. dunant, a swiss philanthropist, founded the red cross.
25. Bill and i asked the ames travel bureau on parker avenue for some travel folders.
26. next friday ms. nancy b. lee will show us a film about switzerland.
27. she took the pictures when she traveled through europe last january and february.

Other Things to Do: Write five sentences about a place you have visited. Use at least one proper noun in each sentence.

Using Commas   9

Supply the missing commas in the following sentences.

Example: Shall we play checkers, dominoes, or chess?

The Royal Game of Chess

1. "You should learn to play chess Ted " said Pam.
2. Ted asked "Is it a game of chance?"
3. "No it is strictly a game of mental skill " Pam replied.
4. "Is it similar to checkers dominoes or backgammon?" asked Ted.
5. Pam said "It is a lot like checkers, but it is more exciting."
6. "A chessboard is divided into sixty-four squares " she added.
7. Pam explained "Each player has sixteen playing pieces."
8. They each have a king a queen bishops knights rooks and pawns.
9. Aren't chess pieces made of plastic wood bone or ivory?
10. Yes and some of the intricately carved ones are very beautiful.
11. I once saw pieces made of brass Ted.
12. "In checkers the pieces are moved in the same manner " Ted said.
13. "Yes but in chess each piece can make a different kind of move."
14. "Do all chess pieces have the same value Pam?" asked Ted.
15. "No they have different values " Pam answered.
16. "The queen is the most powerful and valuable piece " she added.
17. Ted a game of chess is like a battle between two armies.
18. Isn't the object of the game to attack your opponent's king Pam?
19. Yes you try to protect your own king and attack your opponent's.
20. Ted said "In checkers a piece captures an enemy piece by jumping it."
21. "In chess one moves to the square the enemy is on " said Pam.
22. When a piece can capture the opponent's king, the player says "Check!"
23. "The opponent must protect the king " said Pam.
24. Ted a player must protect the king or lose the game.
25. Voltaire Napoleon and Frederick the Great played chess.
26. Pam didn't Benjamin Franklin make chess popular in America?
27. In 1899 an eleven-year-old boy was the chess champion of Cuba Ted.
28. On Saturday May 18 1980 a chess tournament was held at our school.
29. A girl from Detroit Michigan won the tournament.
30. In May 1986 two famous players competed in an exciting game of chess.

Choosing Proper Forms

⚷ 23 d, 25 e, f, 30, 31, 32, 36, 40

In each sentence below draw a line under the proper word in parentheses.

Example: (Its, It's) true that stories can (teach, learn) you many things.

A Swiss Legend

1. Switzerland is (a, an) small country in Western Europe.

2. For hundreds of years Switzerland was ruled (buy, by) another country.

3. The Swiss people struggled (to, too, two) drive out these rulers.

4. (Doesn't, Don't) a legend often grow out of such trying times and struggles?

5. One legend can (learn, teach) us about the spirit of the Swiss people.

6. (Their, There) love of freedom was strong.

7. (There, Their) was a hunter who lived in the forest region of Switzerland.

8. William Tell was famous for his skill with (a, an) bow and arrow.

9. "From 90 meters (300 feet) away he (may, can) knock an apple off a tree," people said.

10. (One, Won) day William Tell and his (son, sun) went to the village.

11. There in the market place they saw a cap that had been (sat, set) on a pole.

12. People who passed (by, buy) would bow to the cap.

13. Tell didn't pay (any, no) attention to the cap.

14. Suddenly (to, too, two) soldiers stopped the hunter and his son.

15. "Everyone (who's, whose) passing this way must bow to the cap," they said.

16. William Tell refused (to, too, two) obey and was arrested immediately.

17. The soldiers (new, knew) about William Tell.

18. The officer in charge wished to see (a, an) example of Tell's skill.

19. He (made, maid) Tell's son stand in the market square.

20. "(Sit, Set) an apple on the boy's head," he ordered.

21. Next he said to Tell, "(You're, Your) to stand across the square from your son."

22. "Use (a, an) arrow to shoot the apple off (your, you're) son's head!" he commanded.

23. Tell pulled (a, an) arrow from his quiver.

24. There was not (no, a) tremble in Tell's hand, but there was fear in his heart.

25. Swiftly the arrow flew (threw, through) the air toward the boy.

26. In the next moment two halves of (a, an) apple lay on the ground.

27. The boy was safe, but Tell was taken away to be put into (a, an) prison.

28. Tell was able (to, too, two) escape from the rulers.

29. He (taught, learned) the people (to, too, two) fight for (there, their) freedom.

30. The rulers were driven away, and Switzerland gained (it's, its) independence.

Writing Sentences   🔑 44, 45

On the lines below write complete sentences, using the groups of words in parentheses.
(Score: 3 for each sentence correctly written)

Example: (the sound of thunder)   *Suddenly the sound of thunder crashed through*

the streets.

Summer Shower in the City

1. (crowds of busy people) _____

   _____

2. (cars, horns, traffic lights) _____

   _____

3. (officer blows her whistle) _____

   _____

4. (street corner vendors) _____

   _____

5. (crackling thunder) _____

   _____

6. (red, blue, and green umbrellas) _____

   _____

7. (stopping for hot soup) _____

   _____

8. (shelter under a store awning) _____

   _____

9. (jumping over puddles) _____

   _____

10. (hurriedly to the bus) _____

   _____

Other Things to Do: Draw one line under the simple subject and two lines under the
simple predicate of each sentence above.

Remembering What We Have Learned

1. Write one declarative, one interrogative, and one exclamatory sentence. In each sentence draw one line under the complete subject and two lines under the complete predicate. **O—** 4, 6 a, 7 a, 8 a, 44, 45

_____

_____

_____

2. List the simple subject and the simple predicate of each sentence above. **O—** 45

Simple Subject   _Simple Predicate_

_____   _____

_____   _____

_____   _____

3. Write one common noun and one proper noun. **O—** 13

_____   _____

4. Write the following sentences as they should be written. **O—** 1, 2, 4, 6 a, 9

"did you go on a trip last summer reggie?" i asked _____

_____

"yes on wednesday june 6 1981 we left for texas" he answered _____

_____

"we traveled through austin houston and dallas" he added _____

_____

5. Write the abbreviations for a day of the week, a month, and a state. **O—** 6 d, f

_____   _____   _____

6. On each line write a sentence using one of the words in parentheses at the left of the line. **O—** 30, 32, 40

(there, their) _____

(teach, learn) _____

(to, too, two) _____

Writing Effective Sentences   🔑 44

Consider carefully the thought you want to express before you write a sentence. Decide whether a statement, a question, or an exclamation will express your thought effectively. Try to avoid weak or awkward sentences when you write.

Read the examples below. Why is the last sentence the most effective for getting information?

Examples: How far away is the post office?

I want to go to the post office.

Do you know where the post office is?

Where is the post office?

1. You have just finished patiently gluing a tiny model. As you are gluing the last piece, you accidentally drop it. Write a sentence that tells how you felt. (Score: 5)

_____

_____

_____

2. You would like to run for class office. Write a sentence that explains why you should be elected.

_____

_____

_____

3. You have been talking in class during the study period. Write a sentence explaining why it was necessary that you speak. (Score: 5)

_____

_____

4. You plan to write to a professor of astronomy to ask where you can find out about telescope lenses. Write a sentence that asks for the information. (Score: 5)

_____

_____

5. Have you ever drawn your fingernails across a chalkboard? Write a sentence that describes your sensations. (Score: 5)

_____

_____

Recognizing Pronouns

A pronoun can be used to take the place of a noun.

Example: *He* likes adventure stories.

A pronoun can also be used in asking a question.

Example: *What* is your favorite story?

Sometimes a pronoun points out a person, place, or thing.

Example: *That* is a book from our school library.

Sometimes a pronoun is used to refer to a person, place, or thing already mentioned.

Example: Daniel Defoe was the <u>one</u> who wrote *Robinson Crusoe.*

Talking About Books

I.   Draw a line under each pronoun that takes the place of a noun. (Score: 5)

1.   Have you ever read the story about Robinson Crusoe?
2.   It was written by Daniel Defoe.
3.   He tells how Crusoe was shipwrecked on a desert island.
4.   We enjoyed the book about Tom Sawyer and Huckleberry Finn.
5.   They have many exciting adventures.

II.   Draw a line under each pronoun used in asking a question. (Score: 4)

6.   Who has read *Alice's Adventures in Wonderland*?
7.   What happened to Alice in the story?
8.   Which is Rocky's favorite character?
9.   Whose copy did Rocky borrow?

III.   Draw a line under each pronoun that points out a person, place, or thing. (Score: 4)

10.   This is a book about John Audubon.
11.   That is a book about migrations of birds.
12.   These are some of Audubon's paintings of birds.
13.   Those are paintings of Western birds.

IV.   Draw a line under each pronoun that refers to someone or something already mentioned. (Score: 3)

14.   Was it Manuel who liked *Julie of the Wolves*?
15.   Misu has loaned me *The Little Prince,* which is her favorite book.
16.   The woman whom you met writes books for children.

Pronouns as Subjects

Draw a line under the pronoun that is the subject of each sentence.

Example: She is the mayor of Chicago.

1. Do you know what mayors do?
2. They serve as heads of their city governments.
3. It is a very challenging job!
4. This is an elected office.
5. Is it our job to elect the mayor?
6. That is the job of every adult citizen.
7. You may know your mayor.
8. I met the mayor of my city yesterday.
9. He is an active and concerned person.
10. He was with Ms. Chiang.
11. She is the deputy mayor.
12. I asked Mayor Clarke what a mayor does.
13. He said that each mayor's task is a little different.
14. It depends on the needs of each city.
15. Do we need better traffic control?
16. That is one of his main concerns.
17. We also need new parks.
18. He is also concerned about our streets.
19. They should be smooth and safe for driving.
20. We have an excellent fire department.
21. It has recommended many changes for fire prevention.
22. He hopes the city council will approve these changes.
23. This is also the mayor's responsibility.
24. He has a difficult job.
25. Must he make many choices?
26. Often it is necessary for him to choose between two good things.
27. He would like to be able to do everything.
28. That is not always possible.
29. We have learned a lot, Mr. Clarke.
30. We thank you for your time.
31. You must be very busy.
32. Then they walked up the steps to his office.
33. Do you know the mayor of your city?

Perfect Score **44**   My Score:

Pronouns for Nouns

On the line at the right of each sentence write the pronoun that could be used in the place of the italicized noun or group of words. (Score: 2 for each pronoun)

Examples: Sue, will *Sue* point to Iceland on the map?   *you*

Charles and I read an interesting book about Iceland.   *we*

The Land of Ice and Fire

1.   *Iceland* is an island in the North Atlantic Ocean.   _____

2.   *Charles* said that it is about the size of the state of Virginia.   _____

3.   Most of *the Icelanders* live at the southern end of the island.   _____

4.   Charles told *Sue* that it is not too cold there.   _____

5.   But Sue told *Charles and me* that it is very cold in the north.   _____

6.   *Sue* showed us the capital city, Reykjavík, on the map.   _____

7.   *The daylight* is almost continuous in the summertime.   _____

8.   But in the winter *the nights* are very long.   _____

9.   In winter early Icelanders enjoyed telling *stories*.   _____

10.   "The stories were called sagas," Charles explained to *Sue*.   _____

11.   Charles said, "Let *Charles* tell about the volcanoes on the island."   _____

12.   *Hekla* is the most famous volcano.   _____

13.   Sue said, "Charles, may *Sue* tell about the boiling springs?"   _____

14.   What are *the boiling springs*?   _____

15.   Icelanders are glad to have *the boiling springs*.   _____

16.   *The people* pipe the boiling water to their homes.   _____

17.   They do not need *water heaters*.   _____

18.   Charles, let Sue tell *Charles* about Iceland's wildlife.   _____

19.   Sue said, "I told *Charles* that seals are almost the only wild animals."   _____

20.   "Yet there are many kinds of birds in Iceland," *Sue* added.   _____

21.   Most of *the Icelanders* farm or fish for a living.   _____

22.   Sonny said, "Please show *Sonny* your stamps from Iceland."   _____

Proper Use of Pronouns

🔑 17 a, b, c, d, e, f

Draw a line under the proper form in parentheses.

Example: Anne and (I, me) were watering the garden.

Garden Insects

1. (We, Us) were standing in the garden.
2. It was (I, me) who saw the beautiful insect.
3. Jason asked (me, I) if I knew the name of the insect.
4. (Jason and me, Jason and I) found a picture of it in a reference book.
5. I told (he and she, him and her) that it is called a lacewing.
6. He showed (we, us) the insect's four lacy wings.
7. Jason said, ''(Them, They) look like spun glass.''
8. He told (I, me) that the lacewing eats many harmful insects.
9. (We, Us) learned that bees, butterflies, and moths are other helpful insects.
10. It is (they, them) that pollinate plants.
11. (We, Us) had read how bees form one of our important foods.
12. Jason and Toni were weeding the garden by (themselves, theirselves).
13. Suddenly Jason called to (we, us), ''Here's a ladybug.''
14. He said to (you and I, you and me), ''This insect is also called a ladybird.''
15. (He, Him) added, ''It helps protect garden plants.''
16. (She, Her) and (I, me) had read that it eats fruit lice.
17. We told (they, them) that ladybirds were brought to California from Australia.
18. (I and Anne, Anne and I) told how they were placed in lemon and orange groves.
19. Without the ladybirds, there might be no citrus fruits for (we, us) to enjoy.
20. Later, Jason showed (Anne and me, me and Anne) a praying mantis.
21. (He, Him) showed (we, us) how the mantis raises its front legs.
22. He said that he (himself, hisself) had found one in his garden.
23. It was (I, me) who said, ''It's a very greedy insect.''
24. ''But it eats insects that destroy plants,'' I said to (they, them).
25. Toni told (I, me) that tumblebugs and bombardier beetles are helpful to people.
26. (They, Them) are called scavengers because they eat decaying matter.
27. Jason said to (she, her), ''Don't ants often damage crops?''
28. ''Yes,'' Toni told (he, him), ''but they also eat harmful insects.''
29. What other insects are helpful to (us, we)?
30. (Jason and I, I and Jason) would like to give a report on helpful insects.
31. ''It surprises (I, me) that insects are so helpful,'' said Ann.
32. ''What interesting creatures (they, them) are!'' she said.

Using *Who* and *Which*

***Who* refers to persons. *Which* refers to things.**

I.   On each line below write the proper word, *who* or *which*. (Score: 12)

Examples: Andrea knows a boy _____*who*_____ has a shell collection.

The collection, _____*which*_____ is a large one, has shells from many places.

Shells and Their Uses

1.   Jackson is the one _____ showed us his shell collection.

2.   There are many people _____ enjoy diving for abalones.

3.   Jackson has a friend _____ went diving for abalones last summer.

4.   The abalone, _____ is found in warm waters, has a beautiful shell.

5.   The friend gave him this abalone shell, _____ came from California.

6.   Abalones are unlike clams and oysters, _____ have two shells.

7.   The abalone, _____ has only one shell, uses it as a "roof."

8.   The abalone has a fleshy "foot," _____ helps it cling to rocks.

9.   The shell has an inner layer, _____ is called mother-of-pearl.

10.   Abalone shells are popular with tourists, _____ buy them for souvenirs.

11.   Factories buy the shells, _____ are made into jewelry or inlays.

12.   Canning factories can abalone meat for those _____ enjoy eating it.

II.   Draw a line under the proper pronoun form. (Score: 11)

13.   It was (he, him) who told (we, us) that shells have many other uses.

14.   Buttons are made from (they, them).

15.   They asked (he and I, him and me) whether lime is made from shells.

16.   In some countries (they, them) are used in building roads.

17.   Jackson explained to (you and me, you and I) that cars soon flatten them.

18.   (We, Us) also learned about a transparent shell found in the Pacific Ocean.

19.   He told (she, her) that it is used for window glass in the Philippine Islands.

20.   Primitive tribes use shells as money in trading among (theirselves, themselves).

21.   (She, Her) said it is becoming hard to find shells on some beaches.

22.   Too many people collect shells for (themselves, theirselves) or to sell.

Choosing Proper Forms

 17, 20, 25, 30, 31, 32, 33, 36, 40

Draw a line under the proper form in parentheses.

Molds and a Wonder Drug

1. It was Heather and (he, him) who showed the class some molds.
2. (They're, There) tiny plants that live on foods and in soil and water.
3. Heather showed us a white mold, (who, which) was growing on bread.
4. (Sum, Some) mold is growing on that fresh lemon.
5. (Here, Hear) is an onion on which green mold has formed.
6. We (learned, taught) about many kinds of molds.
7. Most of (they, them) are harmful to food.
8. But some molds (may, can) help fertilize the soil.
9. Others are used (to, too) flavor cheese.
10. Today we (know, no) of one mold that has greatly benefited people.
11. It was Sir Alexander Fleming (who, which) discovered that it can kill bacteria.
12. Fleming was (a, an) scientist at the University of London.
13. (He, Him) was making a study of bacteria.
14. (One, Won) day in 1928 he found a bit of green mold in his laboratory.
15. It was accidentally (lying, laying) in a dish of bacteria.
16. He soon (learned, taught) that the mold had killed the bacteria.
17. He (knew, new) that he had stumbled on a remarkable discovery.
18. He (set, sat) down and wrote a report about the mold.
19. Soon other scientists joined (he, him) in studying the mold.
20. After several years they (learned, taught) that a medicine could be made from it.
21. It was (they, them) who named the drug penicillin.
22. This (new, knew) medicine could cure many kinds of infections.
23. In 1941 (its, it's) discovery became widely known in the United States.
24. Until that time there (was no, wasn't no) powerful drug to cure certain diseases.
25. The medicine was put (through, threw) many tests that proved its value.
26. Companies found (themselves, theirselves) making large quantities of it.
27. Doctors began using it (to, too, two) cure blood, bone, and eye diseases.
28. Many people's lives were affected (by, buy) this discovery.
29. Penicillin is used to disinfect serious burns, (to, too, two).
30. Scientists continue to search for other medicines that (may, can) be made from molds.
31. Penicillin is (won, one) of the greatest modern medical discoveries.
32. What (knew, new) medicines will scientists discover?
33. What (can, may) we learn by studying science?

Capitalization   ⟿ 1, 2, 3, 4, 5

Draw a line under each word that should begin with a capital letter.

Example: casey said, ''i have been reading an article called 'conservation.' ''

Wildlife Conservation

1.   she said, ''I read that there are many wildlife refuges in the united states.''
2.   Sean said, ''there is a bird refuge near lake turner.''
3.   i saw it when we drove to the lake on thanksgiving.
4.   jane asked, ''why do we need animal refuges?''
5.   sean replied, ''mrs. hughes said that they protect animals from danger.''
6.   ''mrs. hughes has charge of the refuge,'' he added.
7.   casey said that in early times people hunted animals only for food and clothing.
8.   she added, ''the animals' fur kept people warm in the winter.''
9.   but later people began to hunt animals for sport.
10. dan said, ''mrs. hughes told me that many once plentiful animals no longer exist.''
11. so many Carolina parakeets were captured for pets that they finally disappeared.
12. the great auks became extinct in the atlantic ocean.
13. jane said, ''passenger pigeons were also destroyed by hunters.''
14. within forty years the american buffalo were almost wiped out.
15. didn't people begin to protest this slaughter?
16. the american congress passed laws to protect wildlife.
17. the few remaining buffalo were placed in national parks.
18. Now there is a large herd of buffalo in wind cave national park in south dakota.
19. ''didn't the laws stop people from hunting birds for sport?'' asked jerry.
20. ''yes, and people were limited in the numbers they could hunt,'' answered casey.
21. the first bird sanctuary was created by president theodore roosevelt.
22. it was located on pelican island in florida.
23. many citizens, such as edward bok, used their land for animal preserves.
24. mr. bok's famous Singing Tower was built in a bird refuge in florida.
25. jim said that thousands of fish die every year.
26. ''yes, many streams and lakes have become polluted,'' said casey.
27. sean said, ''mrs. hughes told me that many animals are lost in forest fires.''
28. The book park ranger tells about fighting fires and protecting wildlife.

Other Things to Do: Write five sentences about how people can protect animals.
Underline each complete subject once and each complete predicate
twice.

Punctuation

6, 7, 8, 9, 11

Place punctuation marks where they are needed in the sentences below.

Example: Rosa asked, "Mr. McGuire, do you eat here often?"

International Foods

1. Bill said Dad I'm glad you brought us to Alvarez's Restaurant.
2. What a wonderful way to celebrate Bill's birthday! Rosa exclaimed.
3. "Yes Rosa we all like Mexican food " said Tom.
4. Tom said that he was especially fond of guacamole salad
5. "I think tortillas tacos and enchiladas are my favorites " Bill said.
6. "Bill have you ever tried the sopapillas " asked Bill's dad.
7. Bill replied that he had never eaten any
8. Tom exclaimed, What a treat you've missed
9. "We must order some for you to try " suggested Rosa.
10. "What are they " Bill asked.
11. They are delicious, puffy squares of fried bread Rosa explained.
12. I usually eat too many; that's my trouble, Tom laughed.
13. Rosa said Rice and beans we eat at home are prepared like these
14. Bill's dad asked "Do all of you enjoy foods of different countries "
15. Yes I surely do, Tom exclaimed.
16. Well, the rest of you have birthdays, too Bill's dad remarked.
17. "Shall we celebrate each one with food from a different country "
18. How much fun that would be exclaimed Rosa.
19. "That's a great idea Mr. McGuire!" Tom said.
20. Bill's dad said "We might try Italian French or German food."
21. Tom exclaimed "Let's go to Luigi's for my birthday "
22. Since May 1925 Luigi's Restaurant has served delicious Italian food.
23. Bill asked, Will you have spaghetti pizza or lasagna?
24. I may have all three laughed Tom.
25. Rosa asked Where can we find French food?
26. In New Orleans Louisiana Rosa ate at a French restaurant.
27. Bill's dad said that a good restaurant was owned by Mr P J Fleur
28. Rosa asked May we have my birthday celebration there?
29. "Yes we'll have a cake made of French cream puffs " he answered
30. Bill laughed and said that they needed the book International Cooking.
31. Then we can open our own restaurant! Tom exclaimed.

Using the Dictionary—Finding Words

🔑 41 a

I. Arrange the following words in alphabetical order to the first letter.

carpenter	engineer	harpist	aviator	farmer	nurse	instructor
geologist	janitor	doctor	mechanic	banker	lawyer	king

1. _____

2. _____

3. _____

4. _____

5. _____

6. _____

7. _____

8. _____

9. _____

10. _____

11. _____

12. _____

13. _____

14. _____

II. Arrange the following words in alphabetical order to the second letter.

giraffe	gondola	gallon	geography	grain	glacier	ghost	guess

15. _____

16. _____

17. _____

18. _____

19. _____

20. _____

21. _____

22. _____

III. Arrange the following words in alphabetical order to the third letter.

eastern	eagle	eat	each	eaves	earth

23. _____

24. _____

25. _____

26. _____

27. _____

28. _____

IV. Arrange the following words in alphabetical order to the fourth letter.

bandit	banjo	banquet	banana	banner	banish

29. _____

30. _____

31. _____

32. _____

33. _____

34. _____

28

Using the Dictionary—Guide Words
⌐━ 41 b

The guide words at the top of each page in the dictionary help you to find words quickly. The word at the left is the first word on the page. The word at the right is the last word on the page.

I. Below are some guide words and the page numbers of a dictionary where these guide words are found. Underneath is a list of words. Write the number of the page on which each word could be found in the dictionary.

Page 70	Page 71	Page 72	Page 73
rabbit—radish	radium—ram	ramble—rascal	rash—razor

1. radio _____	9. race _____	17. raid _____
2. ranch _____	10. rap _____	18. rattle _____
3. raft _____	11. rake _____	19. rally _____
4. rate _____	12. rare _____	20. ramp _____
5. rack _____	13. raccoon _____	21. range _____
6. rayon _____	14. raw _____	22. raven _____
7. rafter _____	15. raisin _____	23. radiator _____
8. random _____	16. rawhide _____	24. rather _____

II. In Column A below is a list of words. In Column B are the definitions of these words. After each word in Column A write the letter of the definition that fits the word.

A

B

25. grate _____   a. a group of animals

26. great _____   b. learned by listening

27. heard _____   c. without strength

28. herd _____   d. a story

29. tail _____   e. a part of a fireplace

30. tale _____   f. big in size or quantity

31. weak _____   g. a group of seven days in succession

32. week _____   h. the part or side opposite the head

Word Division   🔑 42

I.   Rewrite the following words, dividing them into syllables. Do not divide one-syllable words; place an *X* beside them. You may use your dictionary.

Examples: about ___*a - bout*___   guide ___*X*___

1.	chalkboard	_____	13.	ignite	_____
2.	cannon	_____	14.	invade	_____
3.	circle	_____	15.	jaunt	_____
4.	cracker	_____	16.	landscape	_____
5.	dial	_____	17.	mascot	_____
6.	effort	_____	18.	motor	_____
7.	falcon	_____	19.	ornate	_____
8.	fence	_____	20.	other	_____
9.	gently	_____	21.	ought	_____
10.	greenhouse	_____	22.	percentage	_____
11.	handle	_____	23.	periscope	_____
12.	happy	_____	24.	simplify	_____

II.   Rewrite the following words, dividing them into syllables. Place an accent mark after the accented syllable.

Examples: similar ___*sim' i - lar*___   surprise ___*sur - prise'*___

25.	brother	_____	33.	abandon	_____
26.	confide	_____	34.	expression	_____
27.	devote	_____	35.	headwaters	_____
28.	equal	_____	36.	increasing	_____
29.	florist	_____	37.	ironwork	_____
30.	giggle	_____	38.	latitude	_____
31.	machine	_____	39.	register	_____
32.	planning	_____	40.	volunteer	_____

Recognizing Sentences in a Paragraph

4, 6 a, 44, 48

There are six sentences in the paragraph below. Rewrite the paragraph, adding the necessary capitalization and punctuation. (Score: 3 for each sentence that is correctly written)

Prometheus, the Fire Bringer

an early Greek myth tells about Prometheus, who was given the task of creating human beings this god felt pity for humans, who were weak and cold he decided to risk his life and steal some of the gods' possessions to give to them he brought fire, tools, and language to the mortals Zeus, the ruling god, was angered by Prometheus's action and punished him by chaining him to a mountain finally, after much suffering, Prometheus was freed by Chiron and Hercules

_____

_____

_____

_____

_____

_____

_____

_____

_____

_____

_____

_____

_____

Other Things to Do: Use a reference book to find out about another myth. Write a paragraph about the myth, using complete sentences and putting capital letters and punctuation marks where they are needed.

Making Outlines

When you wish to give a report or tell a story, it is helpful to make an outline, or plan. Making an outline helps you to organize your ideas. It helps you to stay on the subject, to tell each part in the right order, and to express your ideas more effectively.

Below is an outline form for a report. The main topics have been listed. On the blank lines write the appropriate subtopics from the list. (Score: 20)

Hovers in the air   Lands in a small space

Takes off in a small space   Moves backward in the air

Lands vertically   Lands easily

Moves forward in the air   Moves sideways in the air

Takes off vertically   Remains motionless in the air

Operation of a Helicopter

I. Taking off

    A. _____

    B. _____

II. Flying

    A. _____

    B. _____

    C. _____

    D. _____

    E. _____

III. Landing

    A. _____

    B. _____

    C. _____

Other Things to Do: Write the three paragraphs you have outlined. Write complete sentences and use capital letters and punctuation marks where they are needed. If you need additional information to include in your paragraphs, consult a reference book.

Writing Paragraphs

On another sheet of paper write an outline for a factual two-paragraph composition. Then write the paragraphs on the lines below. You may choose a subject from the list below.

My Favorite Place	**My Worst Habit**	**A Good Friend**
I. Where it is	I. What it is	I. What makes a good friend
II. Why I like it	II. How I can change it	II. My own good friend

Superstitions	**If I Were President**	**If I Could Have One Wish**
I. What a superstition is	I. What I would do	I. What it would be
II. Some common superstitions	II. Why I would do it	II. Why I would choose it

Remembering What We Have Learned

1.   Write four sentences. In the first, use a pronoun to take the place of a person's name; in the second, use a pronoun to ask a question; in the third, use a pronoun to point out a person, place, or thing; and in the fourth, use a pronoun that refers to a person, place, or thing already mentioned in the sentence.   ⚷   17, 18, 19, 20

_____

_____

_____

_____

2.   Write two sentences, using pronouns as subjects.   ⚷   16 a

_____

_____

3.   Write three sentences. In the first, use the name of a holiday; in the second, use the title of a book; and in the third, use a direct quotation.   ⚷   1 h, 3, 5, 9 g, 11

_____

_____

_____

4.   Think of four nouns that begin with the letter _f_. Divide the words into syllables, and arrange them alphabetically on the lines below.   ⚷   13, 41, 42

_____   _____

_____   _____

5.   On each line write a sentence, using one of the words in parentheses at the left of the line.   ⚷   17, 20

(he and I, her and me) _____

(who, which) _____

(himself, themselves) _____

(we, us) _____

(one, won) _____

(through, threw) _____

Writing Quotations

⚷ 11, 46

By using direct quotations, you can often make your stories more vivid and interesting. When direct quotations are used in stories, you must begin a new paragraph each time a different person speaks.

Examples: Tracy said that she was excited.   Tracy cried, ''How excited I am!''

Tracy asked whether I was excited.   ''Are you excited?'' she asked.

Tracy thought of how excited she was.   ''My! I'm excited!'' she thought.

I.   Rewrite the following sentences as direct quotations. (Score: 15)

1. Kristy said that an astronaut must have thrilling experiences. _____

_____

2. Roger wanted me to tell him how to get to the skating rink. _____

_____

3. I explained that I had to take my guitar lesson at five o'clock. _____

_____

II.   Rewrite the following sentences as indirect quotations. (Score: 15)

4. Roger asked, ''Did Sammy come to school today?'' _____

_____

5. ''What a good ball game you missed!'' shouted Laurie. _____

_____

6. I said, ''I remember returning the book last Tuesday.'' _____

_____

III.   Rewrite the following paragraph; use three direct quotations. (Score: 20)

Al said that two more players were needed for a soccer team. Lyn answered that the volleyball team needed two more players. Jan said that both sports were a lot of fun. She added that if the games were played at different times, people could be on both teams.

_____

_____

_____

_____

_____

Recognizing Verbs

 21, 45 b, c

In each of the following sentences draw one line under the noun or pronoun that is the simple subject. Draw two lines under the verb.

Example: Jan has an interesting job.

Today's Engineer

1.   Jan Kelman works as an engineer.

2.   Her company builds parts for computers.

3.   Jan finds her work exciting.

4.   Each day Jan does something different.

5.   Sometimes Jan draws plans for new equipment.

6.   She chooses various materials.

7.   She provides important information.

8.   Then her company builds the new equipment.

9.   Engineers do many kinds of things.

10.   Their job is to solve problems.

11.   Electronics engineers also work at Jan's company.

12.   They solve problems having to do with electricity.

13.   All modern computers use electricity.

14.   A chemical engineer solves different problems.

15.   Textile companies need chemical engineers.

16.   They use chemicals in cloth production.

17.   Food manufacturers also employ them.

18.   Civil engineers design large structures.

19.   They help builders of road and water systems.

20.   Planned cities require civil engineers.

21.   Early engineers trained by being apprentices.

22.   Today engineers learn their skills in colleges.

23.   They study various sciences.

24.   Then they use them in their work.

25.   Their training takes several years.

26.   Mathematics is important for engineers.

27.   It solves many complex problems.

28.   Creative engineers find answers for many of today's problems.

Verbs and Verb Phrases

 24 b, 45 b, c

I.   Draw one line under each simple subject in the following sentences. Draw two lines under each verb phrase. (Score: 2 for each sentence)

Example: Many <u>people</u> <u>have studied</u> remains of prehistoric animals.

Prehistoric Animals

1.   These animals were living on earth long before recorded time.

2.   You can see pictures of them in many books.

3.   People have learned a great deal about these early animals.

4.   Dinosaurs had died millions of years ago.

5.   Many kinds of dinosaurs have lived on earth.

6.   Some dinosaurs must have been very small.

7.   But tracks of huge dinosaurs have been found in the United States.

8.   People have discovered dinosaur bones in many parts of the world.

9.   These bones have been uncovered after many centuries.

10.   People have made skeletons from the bones.

11.   The size of these skeletons would amaze you.

II.   Draw one line under each helping verb in the following sentences. (Score: 13)

Example: Long ago gigantic animals <u>could</u> be found on the American continent.

12.   Perhaps you have heard of the saber-toothed tiger.

13.   The bones of a saber-toothed tiger have been found in California.

14.   Sometimes these animals are called saber-toothed cats.

15.   They are named for their long, sharp teeth.

16.   Large ground sloths also were living long ago.

17.   Sometimes a ground sloth was attacked by saber-toothed tigers.

18.   The body of the ground sloth was covered with shaggy fur.

19.   It could sit up on its hind legs.

20.   Tree leaves were eaten by these unusual animals.

21.   The sloth would use its long claws to feed and protect itself.

22.   Models of these animals can be seen in many museums.

Other Things to Do: Write three sentences about how people have learned about prehistoric animals. Draw one line under complete subjects and two lines under complete predicates.

Principal Parts of Verbs   ⊙━ 24

Write the missing principal parts of the verbs listed below. (Score: 1 for each principal part correctly written)

	Present	*Past*	*Past Participle*
Examples:			
	live	lived	lived
	take	took	taken
1.	drag		
2.			learned
3.		raised	
4.	do		
5.	break		
6.			built
7.			chosen
8.		drove	
9.			ridden
10.		thought	
11.			said
12.	make		
13.		spoke	
14.	swim		
15.			brought
16.	wear		
17.		knew	
18.			grown
19.	fly		
20.		drew	
21.	go		

Using *Break* and *Speak*   ⚏ 24

I. Draw a line under the proper form in parentheses.

The Mystery of a Wire

1. Julia showed the class a wire that had (broke, broken) in two.
2. Then she (spoke, spoken) to the boys and girls.
3. She wanted them to guess why the wire had (broke, broken).
4. Julia said that temperature (broke, broken) the wire.
5. Everyone laughed when she had (spoke, spoken).
6. How could temperature have (broke, broken) the wire?
7. But Julia insisted that she had (spoke, spoken) the truth.
8. Everyone listened when Julia (spoke, spoken) again.
9. She said that the wire (broke, broken) during the night.
10. But still no one could guess why it had (broke, broken).
11. ''Was the wire (broke, broken) by hot or cold temperature?'' Erica asked.
12. Julia smiled after Erica had (spoke, spoken).
13. ''Erica is about to guess why the wire (broke, broken),'' she said.
14. Then Julia (spoke, spoken) to the class about the wire.
15. She told how the wire had (broke, broken).

II. Choose the proper word in parentheses to write in each blank.

16. (took, taken)   Julia had _____ the wire outside after school.

17. (wove, woven)   She _____ one end of the wire around a pole.

18. (took, taken)   Then she _____ the other end of the wire to another pole.

19. (wove, woven)   This end of the wire was _____ around the second pole.

20. (took, taken)   Julia _____ care that the wire was stretched tightly.

21. (froze, frozen)   During the night the wire had _____ .

22. (froze, frozen)   As it _____ , the wire stretched tighter and tighter.

23. (froze, frozen)   The wire had contracted as it _____ .

24. (broke, broken)   It had _____ when it could stretch no farther.

25. (took, taken)   Julia _____ the broken wire from the poles.

26. (broke, broken)   She knew why the wire had _____ .

Subjects and Verbs

 45

Draw a short vertical line to separate the complete subject from the complete predicate. Draw one line under the simple subject. Draw two lines under the simple predicate, which is the verb or verb phrase. (Score: 3 for each sentence)

Example: People|have been enjoying music since early times.

Early Music

1. The earliest people had no musical instruments.
2. But songs have been sung for centuries.
3. Early people beat the rhythm with their hands and feet.
4. The first musical instruments were very simple.
5. Sticks were used to beat a rhythm.
6. Two sticks were hit against each other.
7. People tapped the rhythm of the music with these sticks.
8. The drum was another early musical instrument.
9. Drums were made from logs.
10. A hole was carved through a log.
11. An animal skin was fastened over the ends of the hollow log.
12. People could beat the drum with sticks or with their hands.
13. They could beat the rhythm of a song or a dance.
14. Whistles were fashioned from wood or bone many centuries ago.
15. People learned to cut notches in the whistles.
16. They could make different sounds on the instrument.
17. Crude stringed instruments were made.
18. The lyre was a small stringed instrument.
19. It was something like a harp.
20. Other musical instruments were made from reeds.
21. Reeds of different lengths were cut.
22. These reeds were tied together.
23. They formed a kind of scale of notes.
24. Many folk songs told about people's brave deeds.
25. Songs were sung about important events, too.
26. Their children must have learned a great deal of history this way.

Hidden Subjects and Verbs
⚷ 45

Sometimes the subject of a sentence is not one of the first words of the sentence. It may be hidden among the other words. The verb may also be hidden.

Draw a line under the simple subject. Write the verb or verb phrase (the simple predicate) on the line. (Score: 2 for each sentence)

Example: Early <u>people</u> made clothing from things around them.   _____*made*_____

About Clothing

1. Today many materials are used for clothing.   _____

2. Early people often made clothes from animal skins.   _____

3. Sometimes the skins were very stiff.   _____

4. How hard the people worked to soften the leather!   _____

5. In Alaska some Eskimos chewed the leather for hours.   _____

6. In this way the leather was made soft.   _____

7. In hot climates many clothes were made from grass.   _____

8. Perhaps you have seen grass skirts from Hawaii.   _____

9. Was the first material made from cotton?   _____

10. No, linen cloth was used many centuries ago.   _____

11. First, flax fibers were spun into thread.   _____

12. Then the threads were woven into linen cloth.   _____

13. Another wonderful invention was wool cloth.   _____

14. Now people had a material both warm and lightweight.   _____

15. From the spinnings of the silk worm, the Chinese made cloth.   _____

16. For many centuries the Chinese kept their secret.   _____

17. All over the world people wanted the beautiful silk.   _____

18. But only a few Chinese could make the material.   _____

19. Today cloth is made from glass, milk, and wood.   _____

20. Lovely nylon materials are made from coal.   _____

21. Each year amazing new materials are made.   _____

Separated Verb Phrases

 45

A verb phrase may be divided into parts by other words in the sentence.

Draw one line under the hidden simple subject in each sentence below. Draw two lines under each part of the separated verb phrases.

Example: How will conservation change our ways of life?

Homes of the Future

1.   How will houses of the future look?

2.   Many years from now "apartment cities" will probably be common.

3.   Inside the "cities" indoor gardens will often be built.

4.   People will probably live and work inside these cities.

5.   Electric people movers might possibly replace cars.

6.   Will many new materials be used for buildings?

7.   In future homes, the walls will possibly be made of plastic.

8.   Or would you like a house or an apartment with glass walls?

9.   For these walls a special glass would probably be used.

10.   From inside the house you could easily look outside.

11.   But from the outside one could not see inside the house.

12.   In new homes movable walls may someday be found.

13.   With these movable walls a room could, if necessary, be made larger.

14.   How will energy be conserved in the future?

15.   In future homes, solar heating will more often be used.

16.   Could houses be built into hillsides facing south?

17.   This way a home could easily receive the sun's heat.

18.   Enclosed in a solar dome, a house might not need other kinds of heat.

19.   In the future more people will likely work from their homes.

20.   Will working at home save energy?

21.   Connected to a central office, home computers might certainly be available.

22.   With these computers might people shop from their homes?

23.   In today's microwave ovens can a turkey cook in a few minutes?

24.   In the future a kitchen computer will no doubt store recipes.

25.   When the cook is in a hurry, recipes could rapidly be located.

26.   Would you like to operate this machine?

27.   What will tomorrow's telephones be like?

Other Things to Do: Write five sentences about buildings of the future.

Agreement of Verb With Subject

 23

Use a singular verb to tell about one person, place, or thing. Use a plural verb to tell about more than one.

Draw a line under the proper form in parentheses.

Example: Tom (<u>has</u>, have) told us about a famous contest.

The Olympic Games

1. The first Olympian Games (was, were) held in Greece.
2. (Wasn't, Weren't) this festival held almost three thousand years ago?
3. The Olympics (has, have) been held in many different countries.
4. (Isn't, Aren't) they held every four years?
5. There (is, are) contests in many different sports.
6. Many countries (sends, send) their best athletes to the Games.
7. (Doesn't, Don't) each athlete want to win a contest?
8. An award (has, have) been given to each winner in the contests.
9. A country (is, are) very proud when its athletes (wins, win) these awards.
10. (Doesn't, Don't) the Olympic Games include many races?

11. There (is, are) races in walking, running, and swimming.
12. Bicyclists (has, have) also raced in the Olympics.
13. A pole-vaulting contest always (has, have) many interested spectators.
14. (Hasn't, Haven't) this event always been one of the most exciting?
15. (Doesn't, Don't) a contest in high jumping also take place?
16. Everyone waits tensely until each athlete (has, have) jumped.
17. Many people (enjoys, enjoy) watching the swimming events.
18. An American swimmer (has, have) won seven gold medals.
19. A new record in some sport (has, have) often been made at the Olympics.
20. (Hasn't, Haven't) winter sports been included in the Games?
21. Many people (watches, watch) the skating and skiing contests.
22. (Hasn't, Haven't) the game of ice hockey also been included in the Olympics?
23. (Doesn't, Don't) a Scandinavian often win the skiing awards?
24. Usually someone from Norway or Sweden (wins, win) these prizes.
25. The ice-skating contest (has, have) interested many people.
26. People (was, were) thrilled by the figure skating.
27. (Hasn't, Haven't) the bobsledding contests always been exciting?

Agreement of Verb With Subject   ⊶ 23

Draw a line under the proper form in parentheses.

Example: One of the boys (<u>is</u>, are) making static electricity.

About Electricity

1. Electricity (is, are) made in many ways.
2. What often happens when two different materials (is, are) rubbed together?
3. (Isn't, Aren't) a spark of electricity sometimes seen?
4. These sparks (is, are) made by rubbing things together.
5. This kind of electricity (is, are) called static electricity.
6. Gail and Joe (is, are) combing their hair to make static electricity.
7. (Wasn't, Weren't) they using hard plastic combs?
8. A sharp, crackling noise (was, were) heard.
9. The noises (was, were) made by electricity.
10. Maria (was, were) rubbing some silk over a rod of sealing wax.
11. (Wasn't, Weren't) you surprised to see the sparks?
12. There (is, are) Jim shuffling his feet on a wool rug.
13. (Wasn't, Weren't) he supposed to feel a shock when he touched someone?
14. Yes, and he (was, were) likely to be shocked if he touched a piece of metal.
15. (Isn't, Aren't) Janet and Allison standing in a darkened room?
16. They (was, were) rubbing a piece of silk with their hands.
17. The electric sparks (is, are) easily seen in a dark room.
18. Jim said that static electricity (isn't, aren't) used in our homes.
19. Television sets (isn't, aren't) run by just a few sparks of electricity.
20. (Isn't, Aren't) a flow of electricity needed to run a television set?
21. Debby (was, were) showing the boys and girls a dry cell.
22. The dry cell (is, are) often used to make a flow of electricity.
23. Two wires (was, were) connected to the cell.
24. (Wasn't, Weren't) a bell also connected to the wires?
25. The electricity (is, are) made by the dry cell.
26. (Wasn't, Weren't) the wires taking the electricity to the bell?
27. (Wasn't, Weren't) the bell run by the electric charge?
28. The boys and girls (was, were) interested in the dry cell.
29. (Is, Are) it possible to light an electric bulb with a dry cell?
30. Electricity (is, are) a fascinating subject!
31. Scientists (is, are) learning more about using electricity.
32. Electricity (is, are) used everyday in every city.

Contractions

I. Write the contractions for the following words. (Score: 28)

Examples: will not _____ *won't* _____   has not _____ *hasn't* _____

1.	did not	_____	15.	he is	_____

1. did not _____   15. he is _____

2. cannot _____   16. she is _____

3. will not _____   17. it is _____

4. had not _____   18. you are _____

5. should not _____   19. we are _____

6. could not _____   20. they are _____

7. I will _____   21. I have _____

8. you will _____   22. you have _____

9. he will _____   23. we have _____

10. does not _____   24. they have _____

11. we will _____   25. what is _____

12. they will _____   26. that is _____

13. who will _____   27. who is _____

14. let us _____   28. I would _____

II. Draw a line under the proper contraction in parentheses. On the line write the words from which the contraction was made. (Score: 2 for each sentence)

Example: (Isn't, Aren't) Peru a country in South America? _____ *is not* _____

29. Many people (doesn't, don't) know what quinine is. _____

30. (Don't, Doesn't) the medicine come from the bark of a tree? _____

31. The tree (hasn't, haven't) been found in many countries. _____

32. (Weren't, Wasn't) Peruvian Indians the first to use quinine? _____

33. (Weren't, Wasn't) the bark boiled in water? _____

34. (Isn't, Aren't) other countries buying the medicine from Peru? _____

Reviewing Sentences   ⌘ 44, 45

I. Place the correct punctuation mark at the end of each sentence below.

1. Have you read about the travels of Odysseus

2. Many old legends have been told about this Greek hero

3. What amazing adventures Odysseus had

4. Didn't Odysseus fight in the Trojan War

5. Then he began his long voyage home

6. What an exciting voyage it was to be

II. Write *Yes* beside the groups of words below that are sentences. Write *No* beside the groups of words that are not sentences. (Score: 5)

_____ 7. Odysseus landed on the island of the Cyclops

_____ 8. Trapped in the cave of a great one-eyed giant

_____ 9. The giant was going to eat the travelers

_____ 10. Odysseus managed to escape from the island

_____ 11. Sailed away after escaping from the giant

III. Draw a line under the complete subject in each sentence below. Write the simple subject in the blank at the right. (Score: 2 for each sentence)

12. The brave Odysseus sailed to another island.   _____

13. The beautiful Circe lived there.   _____

14. Many wild animals were seen on the island.   _____

15. Those animals had once been men.   _____

16. The evil Circe had changed the men into animals.   _____

17. The clever Odysseus escaped from her by using magic.   _____

IV. Draw a line under the complete predicate in each sentence below. Write the simple predicate on the line at the right. (Score: 2 for each sentence)

18. Odysseus reached his home at last.   _____

19. He had been gone for twenty years.   _____

20. Nobody knew this strange man.   _____

21. Only his old dog recognized the long-lost warrior.   _____

Reviewing Nouns and Pronouns

🔑 13, 14, 16, 17, 18, 19, 20

I. Draw one line under each noun. Draw
two lines under each pronoun. (Score: 19)

1. Have you ever seen porpoises?
2. They are fascinating sea mammals.
3. They live in the Atlantic Ocean and the Pacific Ocean.
4. Sometimes a school of porpoises follows a ship.
5. Who has seen the animals?
6. Joan, who visited in Florida, has some pictures.
7. We saw the pictures of the porpoises.

II. Draw a line under the proper forms in parentheses. (Score: 9)

8. The trained porpoise, (who, which) Joan photographed, did many tricks.
9. Joan told (him, he) and (I, me) that the animal seemed intelligent.
10. It was Joan (who, which) told about the porpoise's tricks.
11. (Me and Carol, Carol and I) saw the mammal leaping from the water.
12. (Her, She) and (I, me) know that one can jump 6 feet into the air.
13. (We, Us) saw a porpoise jumping through a paper hoop.
14. It was (me, I) who saw one pull a wire to make a bell ring.

III. In the blank at the right of each sentence write the proper pronoun to take the place of
the word or words in italics. (Score: 1 for each correct pronoun)

15. *Joan* said that porpoises usually live in groups.   _____

16. Scientists have studied *porpoises* in their natural environment.   _____

17. *These animals* can sometimes be seen along coasts.   _____

18. Jerry asked *Joan* what a porpoise eats.   _____

19. *The animal* eats nine kilograms (20 pounds) of fish a day.   _____

20. Jerry and I hope that *Jerry and I* will see some porpoises.   _____

IV. Write the plural forms of the nouns listed below.

21. inch _____   24. goose _____

22. star _____   25. knife _____

23. berry _____   26. deer _____

Reviewing Verbs   ⌐ 22, 24, 37

I.   Write the missing principal parts of the verbs listed below. (Score: 16)

	Present	Past	Past Participle
1.	_____	learned	_____
2.	drive	_____	_____
3.	_____	_____	broken
4.	choose	_____	_____
5.	_____	gave	_____
6.	build	_____	_____
7.	_____	knew	_____
8.	buy	_____	_____

II.   Draw a line under each verb or verb phrase in the sentences below. (Score: 14)

9.   Most people know the word "pasteurization."

10.   This word is made from the name of a famous scientist.

11.   Perhaps you have heard of Louis Pasteur.

12.   The cause of food spoilage was not known at one time.

13.   For many years Pasteur had studied bacteria.

14.   He had experimented with heat.

15.   Pasteur learned an important thing about bacteria.

16.   Bacteria could be killed by heat.

17.   Then food would spoil much less quickly.

18.   Other important discoveries were made by Pasteur.

19.   One of these was a vaccine for rabies.

20.   Many books have been written about this scientist.

21.   For many years people had laughed at Pasteur's experiments.

22.   But today we are grateful for this man's discoveries.

III.   Write the contractions for the words listed below. (Score: 6)

23.   are not   _____   26.   it will   _____

24.   she will   _____   27.   she would   _____

25.   would not   _____   28.   do not   _____

Reviewing Proper Forms

🔑 17, 23, 24, 25 e, f, 30, 31, 32, 40

Draw a line under the proper form in parentheses.

Animal Ancestors

1. Would you like to (learn, teach) about early animals?

2. (Us, We) have read about the horse's ancestors.

3. Early horses (were, was) about the size of dogs.

4. They (broke, broken) off small shrubs to eat.

5. Kay (spoke, spoken) to us about prehistoric elephants.

6. (Don't, Doesn't) she have a picture of this animal?

7. The picture shows (an, a) animal that (are, is) the size of a cow.

8. We (may, can) see that the animal (has, have) a long snout.

9. This snout was changed (too, to, two) a trunk after many centuries.

10. The home of the first rhinoceros (were, was) North America.

11. (Weren't, Wasn't) camels once found here, (to, too, two)?

12. Julius told (she, her) and (I, me) about the camel's ancestor.

13. (She, Her) and (me, I) knew that the animal was very small.

14. ''(Set, Sit, Sat) down and look at this book,'' Julius said.

15. Kay asked, ''(May, Can) I see the pictures that (is, are) in it?''

16. They will (learn, teach) us what the early camel looked like.

17. The animal had (know, no) hump when it lived in North America.

18. We (taken, took) the book and (set, sit, sat) down to look at it.

19. Julius had (spoken, spoke) to (they, them) about early dogs.

20. People had (took, taken) the dog into their homes centuries ago.

21. Dogs were probably the first pets that (lay, laid) in early caves.

22. Many early animals (froze, frozen) during the ice ages.

23. Animals have been found that were (froze, frozen) centuries ago

24. People studied these remains after they were (broke, broken) from the ice.

25. Kay (laid, lay) a picture of (a, an) kitten on the table.

26. Then she (sat, set) a picture of a saber-toothed tiger by it.

27. ''(Their, There) are (to, too, two) animals of the same family,'' she said.

28. But the saber-toothed tiger (wasn't, weren't) very much like a kitten.

29. (May, Can) you think of other animals that (is, are) members of this family?

30. ''I (can, may) think of (to, too, two) others,'' said Julius.

31. (He, Him) said the lion and the cougar (was, were) members of this family.

32. What else do we (know, no) about animal ancestors?

33. We can (learn, teach) a lot from visiting a museum of natural history.

Reviewing Capitalization and Punctuation   ☞ 1–3, 5–11

Place punctuation marks where they are needed in the sentences below. Draw a line under each letter that should be capitalized.

Miyoshi's *Washington Gazette*

1. Miyoshi's mother was reading the local paper, The valley news.
2. Washington elementary should have a newspaper, Miyoshi thought.
3. Miyoshi asked mr Junero the next day.
4. "What an excellent idea, Miyoshi " Mr. junero said.
5. Why don't you use friday afternoon to get started
6. Miyoshi happily told her friend, frank.
7. Frank I need a reporter, she said.
8. Our paper will be called The washington gazette.
9. "Yes i can help you after school," he answered.
10. On october 12 1984 the work began.
11. Frank interviewed the principal, ms Jefferson.
12. She told frank about the school's plans for thanksgiving day.
13. Miyoshi talked with mr edwards, the school secretary.
14. He told her about the carnival scheduled for washington's birthday.
15. "We could sure use some publicity Miyoshi," he said.
16. miyoshi talked with students about what they would like to see.
17. She spent saturday and sunday at her typewriter.
18. Even her dog, pepper, was excited about her project.
19. "How will you print the paper " uncle Kam asked.
20. Mr. junero said we could use the schools machine on thursday.
21. Everything was ready by wednesday afternoon.
22. how interesting all the articles were
23. Lees drawing of the soccer game was on the front page.
24. The washington gazette was an instant success.
25. the students began to look forward to thursday afternoons.
26. By the end of november, six issues had been printed.
27. On thanksgiving day, what a surprise Miyoshi had
28. She glanced down at The valley news.
29. "Young reporters Scoop school Events," she read.
30. Miyoshi and her gazette had made page one!
31. Her schools news became the local news.
32. Does your school have a newspaper

Remembering What We Have Learned

1. Use one verb to write three sentences. Use a different principal part of the verb in each sentence. ⚷ 24, 44

_____

_____

_____

2. Write three sentences. Enclose the complete predicate in parentheses and draw a line under the simple predicate in each sentence. ⚷ 45 c, g

_____

_____

_____

3. Write three sentences. Enclose the complete subject in parentheses and draw a line under the simple subject in each sentence. ⚷ 45 b, f

_____

_____

_____

4. Write four contractions on the lines below. ⚷ 37

_____   _____

_____   _____

5. On each line write a sentence using one of the verb forms in parentheses at the left of the line. ⚷ 23, 24, 30

(broke, broken) _____

(spoke, spoken) _____

(is, are) _____

(has, have) _____

(enjoy, enjoys) _____

(took, taken) _____

(teach, learn) _____

The key numbers listed at the beginning of each lesson refer to the text material found on the following pages. There are fifty-eight keys, many of which are divided into sections. The rules, explanations, and examples given in the keys, together with the explanations on the lesson pages, make it possible to complete the exercises with little help from the teacher.

In addition to its purpose as a text for this book, the key section can be used as a guide to review language rules or to find help on special language problems.

Capitalization

○— 1 Names

Capitalize:

a. **Names of persons:** *M*ary *A*nn *K*ing; *G*randfather; *A*unt *L*ouisa

b. **Initials of names:** *J. A.* Hill; James *A.* Hill; *J.* Allen Hill

c. **Titles of courtesy or their abbreviations:** *M*r. (Mister); *M*rs. (Mistress—pronounced ''Missis''); *D*r. (Doctor); *M*iss (not an abbreviation); *M*s. (not an abbreviation)

> *Note:* **The titles** *President, Honorable, Governor, Judge, Reverend, Rabbi, Superintendent, Professor, Colonel, General,* **and** *Admiral* **are generally not abbreviated in letters; the title** *Judge* **is never abbreviated.**

d. **Names of pets:** *T*abby; *S*nowball; *P*epper

e. **Sacred names:** *G*od; *O*ur *F*ather; *J*esus; *K*rishna; *A*llah

f. **Days of the week or their abbreviations:** *S*unday; *T*uesday; *T*hurs.

g. **Months of the year or their abbreviations:** *J*anuary; *M*ay; *S*ept.

h. **Names of holidays and special days:** *C*hristmas; *Y*om *K*ippur; *M*emorial *D*ay; *F*ourth of *J*uly (note that unimportant words, such as ''of,'' are not capitalized)

i. **Names of particular places and things:** *E*urope; *C*anada; *M*issouri; *C*leveland *C*ounty; *S*t. Louis; *O*ak *A*venue; *W*ilson *S*chool; *R*ocky *M*ountains; *O*hio *R*iver; *L*ake *E*rie; *C*arlsbad *C*averns; *L*incoln *P*ark; *C*arnegie *L*ibrary; *C*ivil *W*ar; *C*ongress (United States); *R*ed *C*ross; ''*M*ayflower'' (ship)

j. **Words formed from names of places:** *M*exican; *F*rench; *A*merican; *C*hinese

Note: **Names of the seasons should not be capitalized:** *s*pring; *f*all; *w*inter

○— 2 Word *I*

a. **Capitalize the word** *I*: The pencil *I* am using does not belong to me.

○— 3 Titles

a. **Capitalize the first word and every important word in a title or topic:** *T*he *A*dventures *of H*uckleberry *F*inn; *H*ow to *R*epair an *E*ngine

○— 4 Sentences

a. **Capitalize the first word of a sentence:** *D*oes John like to swim? *Y*es, and he likes to dive, too.

○— 5 Quotations

a. **Capitalize the first word of a direct quotation:** Sue said, ''*I* see you understand.'' ''*I* see you understand,'' said Sue. ''*I* see,'' said Sue, ''you understand.''

b. **Do not capitalize the first word of an indirect quotation:** Pete said that he understood.

Note: **For capitalization in letter writing, see Keys 52, 53, 54, and 55.**

Punctuation

🔑 6 Period

a. Use a period at the end of a declarative sentence: The snow was falling softly.

b. Use periods after initials of names:
J. B. Johnson; J. B. J.

c. Use periods after abbreviated titles of courtesy: Mr. Bryan; Mrs. Lane

Note: **Except for *Ms.*, do not use periods after titles of courtesy that are not abbreviations:** Miss Williams; Judge Eastland; Ms. Hunter

d. Use periods after abbreviations of days and months:

Days

Sunday—Sun.	Thursday—Thurs.
Monday—Mon.	Friday—Fri.
Tuesday—Tues.	Saturday—Sat.
Wednesday—Wed.	

Months

January—Jan.	July— (none)
February—Feb.	August—Aug.
March—Mar.	September—Sept.
April—Apr.	October—Oct.
May— (none)	November—Nov.
June— (none)	December—Dec.

e. Use periods after abbreviations of directions:

North—N.	Northeast—N.E.
South—S.	Northwest—N.W.
East—E.	Southeast—S.E.
West—W.	Southwest—S.W.

f. Use periods after abbreviations of states:

Note: **The names of states should be spelled out when they stand alone or follow a city. The first abbreviation that is listed for most states is used most often in lists, maps, footnotes, and bibliographies. The second abbreviation listed is the two-letter, postal form that is used with ZIP codes and has no period following it.**

Examples:

1. Alabama—Ala.—AL
2. Alaska— (none)—AK
3. Arizona—Ariz.—AZ
4. Arkansas—Ark.—AR
5. California—Calif.—CA
6. Colorado—Colo.—CO
7. Connecticut—Conn.—CT
8. Delaware—Del.—DE
9. Florida—Fla.—FL
10. Georgia—Ga.—GA
11. Hawaii— (none)—HI
12. Idaho— (none)—ID
13. Illinois—Ill.—IL
14. Indiana—Ind.—IN
15. Iowa— (none)—IA
16. Kansas—Kans.—KS
17. Kentucky—Ky.—KY
18. Louisiana—La.—LA
19. Maine— (none)—ME
20. Maryland—Md.—MD
21. Massachusetts—Mass.—MA
22. Michigan—Mich.—MI
23. Minnesota—Minn.—MN
24. Mississippi—Miss.—MS
25. Missouri—Mo.—MO
26. Montana—Mont.—MT
27. Nebraska—Nebr.—NB
28. Nevada—Nev.—NV
29. New Hampshire—N.H.—NH
30. New Jersey—N.J.—NJ
31. New Mexico—N.Mex.—NM
32. New York—N.Y.—NY
33. North Carolina—N.C.—NC
34. North Dakota—N.Dak.—ND
35. Ohio— (none)—OH
36. Oklahoma—Okla.—OK
37. Oregon—Oreg.—OR
38. Pennsylvania—Pa.—PA
39. Rhode Island—R.I.—RI
40. South Carolina—S.C.—SC
41. South Dakota—S.Dak.—SD
42. Tennessee—Tenn.—TN
43. Texas—Tex.—TX
44. Utah— (none)—UT
45. Vermont—Vt.—VT
46. Virginia—Va.—VA
47. Washington—Wash.—WA
48. West Virginia—W.Va.—WV
49. Wisconsin—Wis.—WI
50. Wyoming—Wyo.—WY

g. Use periods after other abbreviations: Avenue—Ave.; Street—St.; Boulevard—Blvd.; Road—Rd.; Rural Route Delivery—R.R.D.; Company—Co.; Building—Bldg.

h. If a period comes at the end of a direct quotation, place the period inside the end quotation mark: Catherine said, ''Let me show you my experiment.''

7 Question Mark

a. **Use a question mark at the end of an interrogative sentence:** Have you ever seen a koala*?*

b. **If a question mark comes at the end of a direct quotation, place the question mark inside the end quotation mark:** Harry asked, ''Have you ever seen a koala*?*'' ''Have you ever seen a koala*?*'' asked Harry.

8 Exclamation Point

a. **Use an exclamation point at the end of an exclamatory sentence:** Oh, what a beautiful sunset*!*

b. **If an exclamation point comes at the end of a direct quotation, place the exclamation point inside the end quotation mark:** ''The game is over*!*'' exclaimed Lisa. Connie yelled, ''What a game*!*''

9 Comma

a. **Use a comma between the name of the month and the year:** October, 1492

b. **Use a comma between the day of the month and the year:** December 7, 1985

c. **Use a comma between the day of the week and the month:** Monday, November 18

d. **When a date is given in a sentence, place a comma after the year, unless the date comes at the end of the sentence:** On October 12, 1492, Columbus discovered America. Columbus discovered America on October 12, 1492.

e. **Use a comma between the name of a town or city and the name of a state:** Jill lived in Topeka, Kansas, but she moved to San Francisco, California.

f. **When a city and state or a city and country are given in a sentence, place a comma after the state or country, unless it comes at the end of the sentence:** Did you visit Aspen, Colorado, last year? London, England, is situated on the Thames River.

g. **Use a comma to separate a direct quotation from the words that tell who said it, unless the quotation is a question or an exclamation that comes before the words that tell who said it:** Laura said, ''Let's give a show.''

''I'll build a stage,'' said Rosa. ''Can we make costumes?'' asked Laura.

h. **When you speak to a person in a sentence and call him or her by name, separate the name from the rest of the sentence by one or two commas:** ''Richard, will you erase the board, please?'' ''I'll be happy to, Pete, if I can find an eraser.''

Note: **The naming of the person to whom something is said is called** *direct address.*

i. **When** *yes* **or** *no* **is used at the beginning of a sentence that answers a question, place a comma after the** *yes* **or** *no*: Yes, I saw a shark in the Pacific. No, I didn't see a squid.

j. **Use a comma to separate words or groups of words in a series:** It was a warm, sunny, and bright day. Carlos, Frank, Tina, and I went to the park. We shot baskets, chased each other, and climbed trees. We climbed an oak tree, an elm tree, and a pine tree. Frank fell from his tree, hit the ground, and hurt his arm.

Note: **A** *series* **is a list of three or more words or groups of words naming persons, things, or actions. A series may also be a list of three or more words or groups of words describing something.**

k. **Use a comma after the greeting in a friendly letter:** Dear Aunt Jane,

l. **Use a comma after the complimentary close of a letter:** Very truly yours,

10 Apostrophe

a. **When you combine two words to form a contraction, use an apostrophe (') to show where letters have been left out:** we will—we *'*ll; has not—hasn*'*t

b. **When you form the possessive of a singular word, add an apostrophe and an** *s* **(*'s*):** the book*'s* cover; Jill*'s* book

c. **When you form the possessive of a plural word, add an apostrophe only ('). If the plural does not end in** *s*, **add an apostrophe and an** *s* **(*'s*):** boys*'* pockets; children*'s* stories

Note: **See also Keys 15 and 37.**

11 Quotation Marks and Underlining

a. **Titles of reports, songs, short stories, poems, and other short works are written** with quotation marks in sentences and lists: I like the poem "Windy Nights." We read "Windy Nights" last year. Did you read "Windy Nights"?

b. **Titles of books, plays, magazines, movies, and other long works are underlined:** We enjoyed <u>Charlotte's Web</u>.

Note: Quotation marks or underlining is not used when the title is written above a report, story, or other composition.

c. **Place quotation marks around direct quotations:** Dale said, "Let's play ball." "We won!" Pam shouted.

d. **Do not use quotation marks in indirect quotations:** Pam said that we won.

12 Colon

Use a colon after the greeting in a business letter: Dear Mr. Bruce*:*

Parts of Speech

13 Nouns

a. **A *noun* is a word that names a person, a place, or a thing. Everything that is a noun can act or be acted upon. *Common nouns* are general names:** city; children; boat

b. ***Proper nouns* name particular persons, places, or things:** Jack; Chicago; Lincoln School. **Proper nouns are capitalized.**

14 Plurals of Singular Nouns

A *singular noun* names one person, place, or thing. A *plural noun* names more than one. There are several ways to form plurals.

a. **The plurals of most words are formed by adding *s* to the end of the singular word:** girl—girl**s**; car—car**s**; boat—boat**s**

b. **To form the plural of a word ending in *ch, sh, s, x,* or *z,* add *es* to the singular word:** inch—inch**es**; bush—bush**es**; box—box**es**

c. **For most words ending in *f, fe,* or *ff,* the plurals are formed by adding *s* only:** roof—roof**s**; safe—safe**s**; cliff—cliff**s**

d. **For some words ending in *f* or *fe* the plurals are formed by replacing the *f* or *fe* with *ves*:** shelf—shel**ves**; life—li**ves**; knife—kni**ves**

e. **To form the plural of a word ending in *y* with a consonant before it, replace the *y* with *i* and add *es.* To form the plural of a word ending in *y* with a vowel before it, add *s*:** lily—lil**ies**; baby—bab**ies**; monkey—monkey**s**

f. **To form the plural of a word ending in *o* with a vowel before it, add *s*:** radio—radio**s**; trio—trio**s**; rodeo—rodeo**s**

g. **To form the plural of some words ending in *o* with a consonant before it, add *s*:** solo—solo**s**; piano—piano**s**; pueblo—pueblo**s**

h. **To form the plural of other words ending in *o* with a consonant before it, add *es*:** potato—potato**es**; tomato—tomato**es**; veto—veto**es**

i. **To form the plurals of some words, change the spelling of the singular forms:** man—**men**; mouse—**mice**; goose—**geese**

j. **The spelling of some words is the same for both the singular and the plural forms:** deer—**deer**; sheep—**sheep**; fish—**fish**

15 Possessives of Nouns

A *possessive word* is one that shows ownership, possession, or another close relationship.

a. **To form the possessive of a singular word or name, add an apostrophe and an *s* (*'s*) to the singular form:** Kate*'s* book, Wes*'s* radio

b. **To form the possessive of a plural word ending in *s,* add only an apostrophe. If the plural form does not end in *s,* add an apostrophe and an *s*:** girls' hats; women's hats

16 Pronouns

a. **A *pronoun* is a word used in the place of a noun:** *He* (Jim) went to town (*He* takes the place of *Jim*). *It* (The dog) ran home (*It* takes the place of *The dog*). *They* (Bill and Sue) play records (*They* takes the place of *Bill and Sue*). "Will *you* (Bill) put the record on?" asked Sue (*you* takes the place of *Bill*).

b. **There are four kinds of pronouns: *personal, interrogative, demonstrative,* and *relative.***

17 Personal Pronouns

a. A *personal pronoun* takes the place of a definite person or thing. *I, me, we, us, you, he, him, she, her, it, they,* and *them* are personal pronouns.

b. To tell who did something, use the pronoun *I, he, she, we,* or *they* (not *me, him, her, us,* or *them*): *She* and *I* helped build a hut. Ellen and *he* made the roof. *We* All-Stars have a clubhouse. Pat and *they* ate lunch in the hut.

c. When you tell about others and yourself in the same sentence, place the nouns and pronouns that name others before the pronoun *I* or *me*: Jim and *I* went fishing. Mary, Lisa, and *I* were singing. That dog belongs to Joe and *me.* Dad gave Lee, Sean, and *me* a dollar.

d. After such words as *told, give, heard, from, to, for, by,* or *with,* use the pronoun *me, him, her, us,* or *them* (not *I, he, she, we,* or *they*): Nan told *us* about the game. Joe gave the kite to Ron and *me.* Mary gave the book to *us.* Bob went with Jack and *them.* Jack told *him* to walk fast. The gift is from *her.*

e. After *it is, it was, is it,* or *was it,* use *I, he, she, we,* or *they*: It is *I* who needs that book. It was *he* at the door. Was it *we* who won the game? Is it *they* who found the money?

f. The word *self* is combined with personal pronouns to form *myself, yourself, himself, herself, itself, ourselves, yourselves,* and *themselves*: Carl went to the woods by *himself.* They drew funny pictures of *themselves.* We like to draw pictures of *ourselves.*

g. *Possessive pronouns* are also personal pronouns and are used to show ownership. *My, mine, your, yours, his, her, hers, its, our, ours, their,* and *theirs* are possessive pronouns: *My* name is Sam. The football is *theirs.*

18 Interrogative Pronouns

a. An *interrogative pronoun* is used in asking a question. *Who, what, which, whom,* and *whose* are interrogative pronouns: *Who* is going to the show? *What* is playing? *Whose* ticket is lost?

19 Demonstrative Pronouns

a. A *demonstrative pronoun* is used to point out a person, place, or thing. *This, that, these,* and *those* are demonstrative pronouns: *This* is Lou's notebook. *Those* are her pencils.

b. Use the demonstrative pronouns *this* and *these* to point out persons or things near you: *These* are novels on the shelf beside me.

c. Use the demonstrative pronouns *that* and *those* to point out persons or things away from you: *Those* are my cousins standing over there.

20 Relative Pronouns

a. A *relative pronoun* is used to refer to a person, place, or thing already mentioned in the sentence. *Who, whose, whom, which,* and *that* are relative pronouns.

b. *Who, whose,* and *whom* refer to persons: Toni is the person *who* is going to sing. The boy *whose* shirt was torn is my brother. The man *whom* I saw was wearing a black hat.

c. *Which* refers to things: The plane, *which* was long overdue, finally arrived.

d. *That* can refer to things and to persons: The engine *that* failed finally started again. The pilot *that* (or *who*) flew the plane landed it safely.

21 Verbs

a. *Verbs* are words that show action: The angry dog *barked.* Jack *jumped* over the fence. Juan *laughed* at Jack's torn shirt.

b. Verbs also show being or state of being: Brad *was* in the yard. I *am* old enough. Lila *seems* sad today.

Note: A sentence always has one or more verbs as its *simple predicate.* A sentence can also have other verbs which are not part of the simple predicate: Jack *waited* patiently to *go* to the store (*waited* is the verb that is the simple predicate; *go* is a verb but is not part of the simple predicate). His sister *was* the one who finally *went* (*was* is the verb that is the simple predicate; *went* is a verb but is not part of the simple predicate).

22   Verb Phrases

a. Sometimes a group of words is needed to express the full meaning of a verb. A *verb phrase* is a group of words used to make one verb: The boys *are digging* a cave. Where *are* they *digging* it? Anne *should have gone* home early. The picture *will have been drawn* by now.

b. The words in a verb phrase may be separated by other words in the sentence: Where *are* they *digging* the cave? They *have* already *dug* deep into the ground.

 23   Agreement of Subject and Verb

a. Use a *singular verb* to tell about one person, place, or thing. Use a *plural verb* to tell about more than one person, place, or thing: Lisa *is* (singular) at the store. The girls *are* (plural) in the library. The tree *has* (singular) apples on it. The apples *have* (plural) bright red skins. That man *plays* (singular) the piano. Those two women *play* (plural) violins. One of the kites *was* (singular) in the air. Three others *were* (plural) ready to fly. Each of the boys *goes* (singular) to school. All of them *go* (plural) to the same school. Everyone *likes* (singular) an exciting ball game. *Does* (singular) anyone live here?

b. Use a *plural verb* with the pronoun *you* or *I*: You *are* a good swimmer. I *have* an interesting hobby.
   Note: Two exceptions to this rule are *I am* and *I was*: *I am* ready to try. *I was* not ready yesterday.

c. Use *doesn't* to tell about one person, place, or thing: Iceland *doesn't* have many trees.

   Use *don't* to tell about more than one person, place, or thing: Trees *don't* grow well there.

 24   Principal Parts of Verbs

a. Verbs have three principal parts: the *present*, the *past*, and the *past participle*. The third principal part always needs one or more helping words.

b. *Helping words* are also verbs. Verbs that may be used as helping words are *is, are, been, being, was, were, has, have, had, shall, should, will, would, could,* and *can*: I

have gone to the library many times. The book I want *has been* returned. I *shall* go to the library tomorrow. One of my books *has been* lost. All of my books *are being* lost. I *should have* put them away. Brad *will* help me find them.

Note the principal parts of the following verbs:

Present	Past	Past Participle
become	became	become
begin	began	begun
blow	blew	blown
break	broke	broken
bring	brought	brought
build	built	built
buy	bought	bought
choose	chose	chosen
come	came	come
do	did	done
drag	dragged	dragged
draw	drew	drawn
drink	drank	drunk or drank
drive	drove	driven
eat	ate	eaten
fall	fell	fallen
fly	flew	flown
freeze	froze	frozen
give	gave	given
go	went	gone
grow	grew	grown
have	had	had
hear	heard	heard
know	knew	known
lay	laid	laid
learn	learned	learned
lie	lay	lain
make	made	made
raise	raised	raised
ride	rode	ridden
ring	rang or rung	rung
rise	rose	risen
run	ran	run
say	said	said
see	saw	seen
set	set	set
sing	sang or sung	sung
sink	sank or sunk	sunk

sit	sat	sat
speak	spoke	spoken
steal	stole	stolen
swim	swam	swum
take	took	taken
teach	taught	taught
think	thought	thought
throw	threw	thrown
wear	wore	worn
weave	wove	woven
write	wrote	written

25 Adjectives

a. An *adjective* is a word that points out or describes a noun or a pronoun. An adjective tells *what kind, how many,* or *which one*: I am reading an *interesting* story. George photographed *two yellow* butterflies. Her hair is *short* and *curly.*

b. The words *the, a,* and *an* are also adjectives, but they are called *articles,* since they do not describe or point out.

c. The article *the* is used to refer to a definite person, place, or thing: *The* box in our car is full of food.

d. The articles *a* and *an* are called *indefinite articles,* since they do not refer to a definite person, place, or thing: *A* woman answered the telephone.

e. The word *an* is generally used before a word that begins with a vowel sound. The *vowels* in the alphabet are *a, e, i, o,* and *u. An* is not used before words beginning with the sound of long *u*: an apron; *an* egg; *an* idea; *an* ocean; *an* uncle; *an* hour

f. The word *a* is generally used before a word that does not begin with a vowel sound. It is also used before a word beginning with the sound of long *u*: a unicorn; *a* question

g. A *demonstrative adjective* points out (but does not describe) a particular noun or pronoun by telling which one: *This* book is a mystery story. *That* pencil has soft lead. *These* apples are not ripe. *Those* bananas are ripe.

Note: Sometimes a noun is used to describe a noun or pronoun: Eli enjoys the *mountain* air.

26 Adverbs

a. An *adverb* can explain or describe a verb. It tells *how, when,* or *where* the action takes place. Adverbs may be used to explain or modify adjectives or other adverbs as well as verbs: He writes *well.* Mary came *early.* Paula lives *here.* She is a *very* good scientist. He can draw *unusually well.*

b. Many adverbs are formed by adding *ly* to an adjective: quick—quick*ly*; poor—poor*ly*; gentle—gent*ly*; slow—slow*ly*

c. Do not confuse the adjective *good* with the adverb *well*: John writes *well*; he has *good* handwriting.

d. Be sure to use an adjective to modify a noun or a pronoun and an adverb to modify a verb, an adjective, or another adverb: He spoke in a *soft* (not *softly*) voice. He spoke *softly* (not *soft*).

27 Prepositions

a. A *preposition* is a word used to connect a noun or a pronoun to the rest of the sentence: The book is *on* the table (*on* connects the noun *table* to the rest of the sentence). Jerry has traveled *with* them (*with* connects the pronoun *them* to the rest of the sentence).

b. A *prepositional phrase* is a group of words that begins with a preposition and is used to explain or modify a noun or verb: The book is *on the table.* Jerry has traveled *with them.*

c. If the prepositional phrase explains or modifies a noun or pronoun by telling *which one* or *what kind,* it is an *adjectival prepositional phrase*: The man *in the car* is my father (modifies *man*—tells which one). It was a dog *with shaggy fur* (modifies *dog*—tells what kind).

d. If the prepositional phrase explains or modifies a verb telling *how, when,* or *where,* it is an *adverbial prepositional phrase*: Jerry has traveled *with them* (modifies *has traveled*—tells how). He left *on Tuesday* (modifies *left*—tells when). The book is *on the table* (modifies *is*—tells where).

e. Some prepositions have particular meanings:

into — refers to movement from the outside to the inside of something: Ray went **into** the shed to get a rake.

in — refers to the state of being inside something: He was **in** the shed for a long time.

between — usually refers to two persons or things: The rake was lying **between** the door and the window.

among — usually refers to more than two persons or things: The reward was divided **among** all the people in the posse.

off — means physical separation: The book fell **off** the table.

from — means source or beginning: I expect a letter **from** her.

f. Note how the use of different prepositions can change the meaning of a sentence: The bird flew **into** the trees. The bird flew **over** the trees. The bird flew **behind** the trees. The bird flew **through** the trees.

28 Conjunctions

a. *Conjunctions* **are words used to connect two other words, groups of words, or ideas.** *And, but, or, if, when, after, because,* **and** *while* **are words often used as conjunctions:** Rocky *or* Alice will make the bench. They will sand *and* paint it. Fran will bring the bench to school *and* put pots of flowers on it. *If* the plants are watered, they will grow. The plants are growing now, *but* they will not grow unless they have light.

b. Sometimes conjunctions are used in pairs: *Neither* Gina *nor* Jorges was at home.

c. Use conjunctions to combine short sentences into longer, more interesting ones:

Too many short sentences: Rocky will make a bench. Alice will make the bench, too. They will sand it. They will paint it.

Two good sentences: Rocky and Alice will make a bench. They will sand and paint it.

Too many short sentences: Fran will bring some pots of flowers. She will put the flowers on the bench. The plants are growing now. They will not grow unless they have light.

Two good sentences: When Fran brings some pots of flowers, she will put them on the bench. The plants are growing now, but they will not grow unless they have light.

Too many short sentences: Bill was tired. He was working on a model. He wanted to finish the model. He was trying to cut a piece of wood. He was using a sharp knife. The knife slipped. It cut his finger.

Two good sentences: Although Bill was tired, he wanted to finish the model he was working on. He was using a sharp knife to cut a piece of wood, when the knife slipped and cut his finger.

d. Avoid using too many *and***s. Use shorter sentences and a variety of conjunctions to make your writing interesting and easy to read:**

Too many **and***s:* Sue and Mary made a film and Sue wrote the story and Mary photographed it.

Two better sentences: Sue and Mary made a film. After Sue wrote the story, Mary photographed it.

Too many **and***s:* Paul went to the store and bought some groceries and then he took them home and put them into his knapsack and then he and Carlos hiked to the river and they fished and swam all day.

Three better sentences: Paul bought some groceries at the store. When he took them home, he put them into his knapsack. Then he and Carlos hiked to the river, where they fished and swam all day.

29 Interjections

a. An *interjection* **is a word that expresses strong or sudden feeling. It is usually followed by an exclamation point:** Wow! Linda hit a double! Hurrah! George scored!

Other common interjections are *ah! aha! hi! ouch! good! hurry! quick! whew!*

Word Usage

30 *Teach* and *Learn*

a. To *teach* **means to help someone learn:** Carlos **taught** Mel to speak Spanish.

b. To *learn* means to find out about something or to find out how to do something: Mel wanted to *learn* another language.

31 *May* and *Can*

a. Use *may* to ask or give permission: *May* I go to the show? Yes, you *may* go now.

b. Use *can* to show that someone or something is able to do something: I *can* juggle three balls. A seal *can* swim fast.

32 *Sit* and *Set*

a. To *sit* means to rest or take a seat. The principal parts of this verb are *sit*, *sat*, and *sat*: Please *sit* here. You *sat* here yesterday. I have *sat* in this chair for an hour.

b. To *set* means to put or place something. The principal parts of this verb are *set*, *set*, and *set*: *Set* the box here. Yesterday I *set* the box there. I have *set* it there.

33 *Lie* and *Lay*

a. To *lie* means to rest or recline. The principal parts of this verb are *lie*, *lay*, and *lain*: I told the dog to *lie* down. Then he *lay* down before the fire. He has *lain* there all evening.

b. To *lay* means to place or put something. The principal parts of this verb are *lay*, *laid*, and *laid*: Please *lay* the books on the table. Myra *laid* the books on the table. She has *laid* the pencils beside them.

34 Unnecessary Words

a. Leave out any word that is not necessary to the meaning of the sentence:

Use:	John has a new bike.
Instead of:	John *he* has a new bike.
Use:	The men sang a song.
Instead of:	The men *they* sang a song.
Use:	I have a new book.
Instead of:	I have *got me* a new book.
Use:	He found her.
Instead of:	He *went and* found her.
Use:	Bring the box here.
Instead of:	*Go* bring the box here.
Use:	Where is the box?
Instead of:	Where is the box *at*?
Use:	This baseball is mine.
Instead of:	This *here* baseball is mine.

Use:	She took it off the table.
Instead of:	She took it off *of* the table.
Use:	She covered the leaves.
Instead of:	She covered *over* the leaves.
Use:	Where is he going?
Instead of:	Where is he going *to*?
Use:	They are outside the house.
Instead of:	They are outside *of* the house.
Use:	Let's go home.
Instead of:	Let's *us* go home.
Use:	We returned to town.
Instead of:	We returned *back* to town.
Use:	The word was repeated.
Instead of:	The word was repeated *again.*

35 Expressions to be Avoided

a. Certain expressions should be avoided in speaking and writing:

Use:	Instead of:
those rocks	them rocks
is not, am not, are not	ain't
ate, eaten	et
bought	buyed
heard	heared
dragged	drug
drew, drawn	drawed
grew, grown	growed
knew, known	knowed
might have	might of
should have	should of
couldn't have	couldn't of
ought not	hadn't ought
may have	may of
must have	must of
would have	would of
burst	bursted, bust, busted
born	borned
drowned	drownded
himself	hisself
themselves	theirselves

36 Double Negatives

Words such as *no, not, nothing, never, hardly,* and *scarcely* and contractions made from *not* are *negative words.*

a. Use only one negative word to tell about one thing:

Use:	Joe doesn't have *any* chalk.
	Joe has *no* chalk.
Instead of:	Joe doesn't have *no* chalk.

Use:	I haven't bought **anything.**
	I have bought **nothing.**
Instead of:	I haven't bought **nothing.**
Use:	None of them **were** here.
	No one **was** here.
Instead of:	None of them **weren't** here.
	Not no one was here.
Use:	Ann has **never** seen ducks.
	Ann hasn't **ever** seen ducks.
Instead of:	Ann has never seen **no** ducks.
	Ann hasn't **never** seen ducks.
Use:	He **can** hardly walk.
Instead of:	He **can't** hardly walk.

37 Contractions

a. A *contraction* is a verb combined with a pronoun or the word *not* to make a single word. Contractions help make writing sound more natural.

b. Use an apostrophe to show where letters have been left out of a contraction:

are not—aren't	she will—she'll
cannot—can't	she would—she'd
could not—couldn't	should not—shouldn't
did not—didn't	that is—that's
does not—doesn't	they are—they're
do not—don't	they have—they've
had not—hadn't	they will—they'll
has not—hasn't	they would—they'd
have not—haven't	was not—wasn't
he is—he's	we are—we're
he will—he'll	we have—we've
he would—he'd	we will—we'll
I am—I'm	we would—we'd
I have—I've	were not—weren't
I will—I'll	what is—what's
I would—I'd	who is—who's
is not—isn't	who will—who'll
it is—it's	will not—won't
it will—it'll	would not—wouldn't
it would—it'd	you are—you're
let us—let's	you have—you've
she is—she's	you will—you'll
	you would—you'd

38 Synonyms

a. *Synonyms* are words that mean the same or nearly the same thing:

big—large
brilliantly—brightly

cautious—careful
clever—expert, skillful
clumsy—awkward
commonly—generally, usually
conveniently—easily
correct—accurate
enthusiastically—eagerly
far—distant
fast—rapid, quick
fine—excellent
friendly—amicable
hard—difficult
interesting—absorbing
little—small
main—principal
many—several
maybe—perhaps
nearly—almost
odd—strange, peculiar
oddly—strangely
practiced—skillful, expert
quiet—silent
really—truly, certainly
rightly—correctly, accurately
round—circular
somewhat—rather
very—extremely
well-liked—popular

39 Antonyms

a. *Antonyms* are words that have opposite meanings:

add—subtract	awkward—graceful
after—before	buy—sell
ashamed—proud	kind—cruel, unkind

40 Homophones

a. *Homophones* are words that sound alike or almost alike but have different meanings and different spellings.

b. When you use a homophone, be sure to spell the word that gives the meaning you intend:

be, bee	new, knew
buy, by	no, know
died, dyed	one, won
for, four	our, hour
great, grate	sea, see
hear, here	some, sum
its, it's	son, sun
made, maid	their, there, they're

through, threw
to, too, two

who's, whose
your, you're

Using the Dictionary

A dictionary is used to find the definition of a word, its part of speech, and its spelling, pronunciation, and syllable division.

41 Finding Words

a. Words in a dictionary are arranged so that their first letters are in the order of the alphabet. Words beginning with the same first letter are arranged according to the second and following letters:

*an*telope	*ma*de
*as*hes	*mi*lk
*b*ell	*n*est
*c*otton	*ok*ra
*d*ollar	*ow*l
*ea*r	*p*arrot
*ey*e	*q*uail
*fa*ther	*r*adio
*fe*ather	*saili*ng
*fi*re	*sailo*r
*gi*nger	*ti*ger
*gl*ass	*tu*lip
*ha*wk	*u*mbrella
*ho*bby	*v*iolin
ice	*wind*
icy	*wint*er
*j*anitor	*yea*r
*la*wn	*yes*terday
*le*opard	*z*ebra

b. There are two *guide words* at the top of each dictionary page. They indicate that those two words and all words that can be arranged alphabetically between them appear on that page.

42 Dividing Words Into Syllables

a. To aid in pronunciation and writing, words in a dictionary are divided into *syllables.* A syllable may be made up of a vowel by itself, a vowel plus one or more consonants, or one or more consonants without a pronounced vowel: *e-nough; know-ing; can-dle*

b. When it is necessary to divide a word at the end of a line, divide it only between syllables; never divide a word of one syllable: *man* (one syllable); *broth-er* (two syllables); *tel-e-phone* (three syllables); *ed-u-ca-tion* (four syllables); *al-pha-bet-i-cal* (five syllables)

c. Words may be divided between double consonants: *lit-tle; din-ner*

d. Words may be divided between consonants that are not alike: *bas-ket; win-dow*

e. Words may be divided between a vowel and a consonant in order to place a vowel in each syllable: *la-bor; ta-ble*

f. Words may be divided between two vowels: *du-et; ra-di-o*

g. The syllable that is given the most stress when the word is spoken is shown by an accent mark (´): pa´per

h. When you are unsure of the division of a word, check it in a dictionary.

43 Spelling Words

a. When you are uncertain of the spelling of a word, check it in a dictionary.
   See also Keys 14, 15, 37, and 40.

Writing

44 Sentences

a. A *sentence* is a group of words that makes sense. It feels complete when you say it or write it: That is an oak tree. Is it an old tree?

Below are groups of words that are not sentences. Each group has something missing and does not make sense:

An angrily buzzing bee
Flew here and there

b. A sentence that tells something is called a *declarative sentence*: The raccoon is an odd animal.

c. A sentence that asks something is called an *interrogative sentence*: Does the raccoon always wash his food?

d. A sentence that shows surprise or sudden fear or excitement is called an *exclamatory sentence*: What a beautiful rainbow!

e. Do not use too many short sentences. Often two or more sentences can be combined to make one interesting sentence:

Too many short sentences: Presley has a ball. It is new. She has a bat. It is new. She has a glove. It is old.

One better sentence: Presley has a new ball, a new bat, and an old glove.

45 Subjects and Predicates

a. In order to be complete, a sentence should have a *subject* and a *predicate.*

b. The *simple subject* is the single noun or pronoun that the sentence is about: The **man** has gone down the street. Did **you** see Mary?

c. The *simple predicate* is the single verb or verb phrase that expresses the action or state of being concerning the subject: The woman **has gone** down the street. **Did** you **see** Mr. Acosta?

d. A simple subject may be *compound*—that is, made up of two or more nouns or pronouns joined by a conjunction: *Jason and Mona* are going to the supermarket.

e. A simple predicate may also be *compound*—that is, made up of two or more verbs joined by a conjunction: The actress *sang and danced.*

f. The *complete subject* consists of the simple subject and all the words that tell about the simple subject: *The man with the dog* has gone down the street.

g. The *complete predicate* consists of the simple predicate and all the words that tell about the simple predicate: The man with the dog *has gone down the street.*

h. The subject usually comes near the beginning of a sentence, and the predicate usually comes after it. But sometimes their positions are reversed, or they are hidden among other words: There **are** many **crows** in the park. Happy **were** the **days** of my childhood. When the horn sounds, the **game will be** over.

46 Quotations

a. *Direct quotations* are the exact words thought, spoken, or written by someone. Use a capital letter to begin the first word of a direct quotation. Place quotation marks at the beginning and end of a direct quotation: Lill said "Joan went home." "Joan went home," said Lill.

b. *Indirect quotations* tell what someone thought, said, or wrote but are not the exact words. Quotation marks are not used with indirect quotations: Bill said that Jack went home.

47 Outlines

Plan a report or a story by making an outline of what you wish to say. An *outline* is a plan in skeleton form. It shows the main ideas you wish to tell about and the order in which they will be told. Each paragraph is represented by a roman numeral and a statement of the main idea of the paragraph. Following the roman numeral, capital letters and headings show what you wish to tell about the subject of the paragraph. Note the arrangement of the subject and main ideas in the following outline:

Title:
Making and Flying Your Own Kite
Main idea of first paragraph:
I. The fun of kites
  A. Flying kites in the spring
  B. Designing, making, and experimenting with kites
Main idea of second paragraph:
II. Making a diamond kite
  A. Designing a diamond kite
  B. Gathering materials
  C. Making the kite
Main idea of third paragraph:
III. Flying the kite
  A. Finding a good field on a windy day
  B. Staying away from power lines
  C. Trying some tricks with your kite

48 Paragraphs

Most stories, letters, and reports are divided into parts. Each part is called a *paragraph.* A piece of writing may be short enough to be written in one paragraph. Each paragraph tells one thing about the subject. When another idea is developed, it should be written in a new paragraph.

a. A paragraph is made up of one or more sentences that tell about one thing:

> The wren is a small gray, brown, and white bird. It always keeps busy. Its beautiful song makes it welcome in our backyard.

b. Follow these rules in writing a paragraph:

1. Begin the first word and each important word in the title with a capital letter.
2. Indent the first line of each paragraph. ***Indent*** means to begin the first line about 2½ centimeters (1 inch) to the right of the left margin. Begin all other lines in the paragraph at the margin.
3. Leave margins about 2½ centimeters (1 inch) wide at the top, at the bottom, and on each side of the paper. Keep these margins as straight as you can.
4. Begin the paragraph with an interesting sentence that introduces the subject. In other sentences tell more about the subject.
5. Begin each sentence with a capital letter and end it with the correct punctuation mark.
6. Be sure that you have used complete, correct sentences.
7. End the paragraph with a final sentence about the subject.
8. Begin a new paragraph each time you introduce a new idea.

49 Reports

Making a report **is writing about something you saw, heard, read, or did. The thing you write about is the *subject* of the report.**

a. Choose a subject that is interesting and worthwhile.

1. Will the report help the readers learn something they will like to know?
2. Limit your subject. "Soap" is not a good subject because you cannot tell everything about all kinds of soap. "How Pioneers Made Soap" is a good subject because you can tell all the important facts.

b. Plan your report before you write it.

1. Ask yourself questions about the subject. The questions will help you select interesting and important ideas to write.
2. Find important information about your subject in reference books.
3. Write only those ideas that are needed to tell about your subject.
4. Make an outline to arrange your report in logical order.
5. Be sure that you have covered your subject completely in the outline.

c. Write your report neatly and correctly.

1. Begin the report with an interesting sentence that introduces the subject. Tell more about the subject in each of the following sentences. Write a title that will make other people want to read your report.
2. Write neatly, so that your words are easy to read.
3. Proofread the finished report for spelling, capitalization, and punctuation.
4. Read your report to find out whether another person is likely to understand what you want to say.

50 Notices and Announcements

Sometimes information needs to be given to a large number of people. Then a *notice* must be written to be read aloud, placed on a bulletin board, or sent to the interested persons.

a. In an announcement or notice be sure to include all necessary information. Tell what the event is, when and where the event will be held, who may attend, and who is presenting the event:

> The sixth grade will have an art and photography exhibit in their room after school on Monday, January 15. Everyone is invited to see the exhibit.

51 Stories

A *story* tells something that happens to a person or a thing. The people or things told about may be real or imaginary. Usually a story tells about a problem and how it is solved. Most stories have more than one paragraph.

a. Plan the story before you write it.

1. Think of a problem and its exciting or interesting solution.

2. Decide what you must tell about your story so that the reader will understand it. Leave out any idea not needed to tell the story.

3. Arrange the events of the story in the order in which they happen.

4. Make an outline of the story, showing the content of each paragraph, and be sure that you are satisfied with the plan before you begin to write the story.

b. Write the story in an interesting and correct way.

1. Write an interesting title in the center of the first line.

2. Write an interesting sentence to begin the story.

3. Tell all the important events in the order in which they happen.

4. When you tell something new, put it in a new paragraph.

5. Try to use words that say exactly what you mean.

6. Be sure that the last sentence ends the story in an interesting and satisfying way.

c. Check your story after it is written.

1. Have you told everything necessary for a reader to understand the story? Have you told anything that you do not need to tell?

2. Look for short, choppy sentences, and combine them.

3. Proofread the spelling, punctuation, and capitalization in your story.

4. Make sure that your writing is neat and easy to read.

52 Writing Addresses

a. An *address* tells where a person lives or receives mail. A person living in a city usually has a street address. The ZIP code follows the name of the state. If a person lives in a small town, often his or her address is just the name of the town and state where he or she lives or receives mail. A person who lives in the country may have a rural free delivery route number instead of a street address. R.R. is the abbreviation for *Rural Route.*

Mr. Roy M. Ross   Miss Eva Hill
38 Owens Street   P.O. Box 317
Plano, Texas 75074   Tiro, Ohio 44807

Mr. B. D. Arnt
R.R. 1
Crewe, Virginia 23930

b. In an address begin all words, abbreviations, and initials with capital letters. Place a period after any abbreviation.

c. Use a comma to separate the name of a city from the name of a state if they are on the same line in an address. The space of two letters should be left between the name of the state and the ZIP code.

Barre, Vermont 05641

Albany, Oregon 97321

d. When a person's address is written in a sentence, put a comma between each of the following: the person's name and the street address, the street address and the name of the city, the name of the city and the name of the state, and the name of the state and the rest of the sentence (unless the name of the state comes at the end of the sentence):

Send the letter to Ms. Jill Collins, 920 Carson Avenue, Oakland, California 94705, and you will receive an immediate answer.

e. Two-letter state abbreviations may be used in addresses. Both letters are capitalized, and no period follows.

Note: **See Key 6 for a list of the two-letter abbreviations.**

53 Addressing Envelopes

a. Write the name and address of the sender in the upper left corner of the envelope.

b. In the center of the envelope write the title of courtesy, the name, and the address of the person who is to receive the letter. Place a comma between the name of the city and the name of the state only if they are written on the same line:

Cecil Howe
R.R. 3
Lyons, New York 14489

          Miss Ann Lewis
          41 Ashley Drive
          Buhl, Idaho 83316

🔑 54 Writing Friendly Letters

A *friendly letter* is an informal letter written to a friend or relative. It may be written to send a personal message, a thank-you for a gift or kindness, or an invitation to a social event.

a. A friendly letter has five parts:

1. The **heading** gives the address of the person writing the letter and the date the letter is written.
2. The **greeting** tells to whom the letter is written and greets that person.
3. The **body,** or **main part,** gives the writer's message. It is written in paragraph form.
4. The **complimentary close** is a polite or affectionate way to say goodbye.
5. The **signature** is the name of the writer.

b. Follow these rules for capitalization in a friendly letter:

1. In the heading begin all words with capital letters.
2. Begin the first word of the greeting with a capital letter.
3. Begin all names and all sentences with capital letters.
4. Begin the first word of the complimentary close with a capital letter.

c. Follow these rules for punctuation in a friendly letter:

1. In the heading place a comma between the name of the city and the name of the state, and between the day of the month and the year.
2. Place a comma after the greeting.
3. End each sentence with the correct punctuation mark.
4. Place a comma after the complimentary close.

d. Follow this form for a friendly letter:

Heading:
633 Dauphine Street
New Orleans, Louisiana
February 3, 2007

Greeting: Dear Fredrica,

Body:
Mom and Dad gave me a bike for my birthday. It's really a beauty!
I want to try my new bicycle in the open country. Let's ride our bicycles in Audubon Park next Sunday.

Complimentary close: Your friend,
Signature: Dawn

🔑 55 Writing Business Letters

a. A business letter has six parts:

1. A business letter has the five parts of a friendly letter and in addition an **inside address,** which gives the title of courtesy and the name and address of the person to whom the letter is written. A company's name may be used instead of a title of respect and a person's name.

b. Follow these rules for capitalization in a business letter:

1. In the inside address begin all words, abbreviations, and initials with capital letters.
2. Follow the same rules for capitalization of the heading, greeting, body, complimentary close, and signature as in a friendly letter.

c. Follow these rules for punctuation in a business letter:

1. Place a colon (:) after the greeting of a business letter.
2. In the inside address place a period after an abbreviated title of courtesy. Place a comma between the name of the city and the name of the state.
3. Follow the same rules for punctuating the heading, body, and complimentary close as in a friendly letter.

d. Follow this form for a business letter:

Heading:
284 Starbuck St.
Rockport, Indiana 47635
January 24, 2007

Address:
Green Lizard Hobby Company
4486 North Appleton Street
Chicago, Illinois 60610

Greeting: Dear Sir or Madam:

Body:
Please send me a copy of your latest catalog. Enclosed is seventy cents for postage.

Complimentary close: Very truly yours,
Signature: Erica Minelli

Speaking and Listening

🔑 56 Speaking and Listening to Other People

a. Make a report interesting by following these suggestions:

1. Choose an important subject.
2. Decide what you will say about your subject.
3. Write an interesting beginning sentence.
4. Be sure that every sentence tells about the subject.
5. Speak clearly, correctly, and confidently.

b. **Listen carefully to others when they talk, tell stories, or give reports.**

1. Look at the speaker so that he or she will know you are listening.
2. Decide what you should gain from the talk. Are you listening for fun, or are you listening to learn something?
3. Listen to discover the subject of the talk.
4. Listen to decide which of the speaker's ideas are important enough to remember.
5. Think of questions to ask after the talk, but do not interrupt while someone is speaking.
6. Decide which things the speaker did well. Did he or she express ideas so that they were easily understood? Was the talk interesting? Did he or she speak clearly?

57 Recognizing Different Ways to Speak

Many different languages are spoken on earth. Each of these languages can be spoken in a variety of ways, called dialects. English, for example, has hundreds of dialects. In the United States, different dialects are spoken by people from different parts of the country. Even within a single neighborhood, there may be several ways of speaking.

Some people at your school may speak a dialect different from yours. All the dialects that you hear are part of our language, and one dialect is not better than another. In school, however, we learn a common way of speaking. It is important that we master this common, shared dialect so that we may be easily understood by anyone who speaks our language.

58 Broadcasting

Broadcasting means talking about the pictures you see in this book and the many interesting things you see around you in the world. Before you broadcast, look carefully and think.

Broadcasters on television and radio tell people about some things that are happening all over the world, both near us and far away.

When you broadcast in this book, it means that you ask and try to answer questions about various subjects. Talking about new ideas can be fun and you can learn something too.

What kinds of questions can you ask about the pictures and the world? Here are some of them:

What do you see?
What is happening?
Whom do you see?
What are they doing?
Why are they doing it?
Have you ever done that?
How are they feeling? Why?
How would you feel? Why?
What are they saying?
What do you think will happen next?
What other questions could you ask about *each* separate picture?
What kinds of questions could you ask about other things?

Writing a Story

📌 47, 51

On a separate sheet of paper make an outline of a story you would like to write. Then write your story on the lines below. Be sure to give your story an interesting title. Use another sheet of paper if you need more room. Here is a list of some topics that may give you an idea for your story.

A helicopter ride   A make-believe invention

A magical city   A hot air balloon ride

Winning a championship   A rodeo

A trip into the past   Shipwrecked on an island

An ocean voyage   Running in a marathon

_____

_____

_____

_____

_____

_____

_____

_____

_____

_____

_____

_____

_____

_____

_____

_____

_____

_____

Recognizing Adjectives

0— 25

An *adjective* describes or points out a noun or a pronoun.

Examples: a *delicious* apple   the *large red* sign   *that* boy

On the line at the right of each sentence write the adjective that describes the noun in italics in each sentence. Do not include the articles *a, an,* and *the.*

Example: Interesting *things* can be seen on a hike.   *interesting*

1.   The class looked forward to an exciting *hike.* _____

2.   Sam saw a round *nest* hanging from a tree. _____

3.   It was a hornet's nest made of gray *paper.* _____

4.   ''In cold *weather* we can inspect the nest,'' said Wendy. _____

5.   The hikers found interesting *combs* inside the nest. _____

6.   They walked beside a small *creek.* _____

7.   ''Look at the streak across this flat *rock,*'' called Paul. _____

8.   ''The silver *trail* of mucus was made by a slug,'' he said. _____

9.   The mucus enables the slug to crawl across rough *surfaces.* _____

10.   It can crawl safely across the sharp *edge* of a knife blade. _____

11.   A tiny *ridge* of earth appeared at Paul's feet. _____

12.   Something was digging through the soft *ground.* _____

13.   ''A mole may be making this *ridge,*'' said Suki. _____

14.   The curious *hikers* ran to the mound of earth. _____

15.   They watched the mole dig in the moist *dirt.* _____

16.   Soon they could see inside the small *tunnel.* _____

17.   But only the animal's pink *tail* could be seen. _____

18.   The furry *animal* was disappearing into the tunnel. _____

19.   On the long *walk* home everyone was tired but happy. _____

Other Things to Do: Write ten sentences about a camping trip. Draw a line under each adjective you use.

Using Adjectives

 25

Draw a line under each of the adjectives in the sentences below. Do not underline the articles *a, an,* and *the.* (Score: 1 for each adjective underlined)

Japan

1. Japan is a small country made up of many islands.
2. It has four main islands.
3. Throughout the country are beautiful mountain ranges.
4. The majestic peak of Mt. Fuji is the highest point in Japan.
5. Thick forests cover much land in this country.
6. Northern Japan has short, cool summers and long, snowy winters.
7. This modern country has many busy cities.
8. A great number of people live in Japan.
9. Japan produces many manufactured goods.
10. The latest electronic equipment is often made in Japan.
11. Many new ships, cars, and bicycles are produced each year.
12. There is little land for farming in this tiny country.
13. Few animals are raised for food.
14. Much food is found in the ocean.
15. Small fishing villages are found throughout Japan.
16. Some food is sent to other countries.
17. Fresh fish has always been a favorite food of the Japanese people.
18. Both raw and cooked fish are enjoyed.
19. Crisp vegetables are served at most meals.
20. Rice is another popular food in Japan.
21. Large rice fields can be seen throughout the country.
22. Sometimes a dark, brown sauce is put over rice or fish.
23. This delicious sauce is called soy sauce.
24. Japan is an old country.
25. It has a rich, artistic heritage.
26. Samples of ancient architecture can still be seen in the country.
27. Ancient Japanese art is found in modern museums.
28. Japan is known for beautiful textiles and unusual ceramics.
29. Most school children learn about the strong traditions in Japan.
30. They may dress in native costumes for special occasions.
31. Japanese customs are also studied by American students.
32. Have you seen a film about the interesting culture of Japan?

Choosing Synonyms

🔑 25, 36

In each sentence below is an adjective in italics. Replace it by choosing a synonym from the following list and writing it on the line at the right of the sentence.

principal	absorbing	accurate
several	expert	popular
unusual	ancient	swift
circular	skillful	large
silent	awkward	small
careful	excellent	difficult

Archery

1. Today, archery is a *well-liked* sport. _____

2. Many *odd* bows have been used by different people. _____

3. Some of the bows were large and *clumsy*. _____

4. Two *main* kinds of bows are used. _____

5. A straight bow is *fine* for this sport. _____

6. The recurved bow is an *old* Turkish design. _____

7. Sometimes *practiced* archers enter tournaments. _____

8. This *interesting* sport requires great skill. _____

9. The *quiet* archer aims the arrow at the target. _____

10. If the aim is *correct*, the arrow will hit the mark. _____

11. A *clever* archer is good at clout shooting. _____

12. A *big* target is drawn on the ground. _____

13. Usually the target is *round*. _____

14. It is *hard* to hit this target. _____

15. In the center of the target there may be a *little* flag. _____

16. The archer stands *many* yards from the target. _____

17. The archer takes *cautious* aim toward the sky. _____

18. When the *fast* arrow falls, it lands on the target. _____

Possessive Nouns and Pronouns   ⚿ 10, 15, 17 g

I.   Write the possessive forms of the nouns listed below.

Examples: kittens _____*kittens'*_____   Charles   _____*Charles's*_____

1.	fox	_____	8.	James	_____
2.	Ross	_____	9.	friends	_____
3.	chief	_____	10.	cat	_____
4.	boys	_____	11.	Bess	_____
5.	girls	_____	12.	children	_____
6.	Jane	_____	13.	babies	_____
7.	oxen	_____	14.	pony	_____

II.   Write the possessive pronouns that refer to the italicized nouns or pronouns.

Examples: *They* said that the book was _____*theirs*_____ .

            The *book* was returned to _____*its*_____ owners.

15.   *Cathy and Greg* asked _____ mother to visit the school.

16.   *We* have been studying space travel in _____ room.

17.   *Greg* said that the model of a space craft was _____ .

18.   *I* believe that this drawing is _____ .

19.   *Cathy* said that the model of the planets was _____ .

20.   *She* said that the scrapbook was also _____ .

21.   Did *you* say that the exhibit of pictures is _____ , Greg?

22.   *Sue and Sally* said that the exhibit was _____ .

23.   Will *you* read _____ story to us, Cathy?

24.   It is about a *woman* and _____ adventures on the moon.

25.   Later *I* shall give _____ report about Saturn.

26.   This picture of *Saturn* shows _____ rings.

27.   *Cathy* asked _____ mother if she enjoyed the class visit.

Using *A* and *An*

⚿ 25 d, e, f, 40

I. Draw a line under the proper word in parentheses.

Interesting Spiders

1. Have you ever seen (a, an) trap-door spider?
2. This spider builds (a, an) interesting home.
3. First it digs (a, an) tunnel in the ground.
4. Then the spider makes (a, an) mixture of saliva and dirt.
5. This mixture is (a, an) excellent cover for the walls of the tunnel.
6. After covering the walls, the spider has (a, an) waterproof house.
7. The tunnel has (a, an) opening to the outside.
8. But the spider builds (a, an) unusual door for the opening.
9. It builds (a, an) movable door to fit the hole.
10. Often (a, an) energetic spider puts leaves or sticks near the door.
11. It is almost (a, an) impossibility to find the door from the outside.
12. (A, An) enemy has (a, an) hard time finding the tunnel.
13. As it grows bigger, the spider needs (a, an) larger home.
14. It has (a, an) easy time making the tunnel larger.
15. (A, An) small piece of the wall is scraped off and carried away.
16. In (a, an) hour or so the spider has (a, an) useful, larger home.

II. Draw a line under the proper word in parentheses.

17. (There, Their) is another curious spider called the "bolas spider."
18. (It's, Its) a large spider found in many parts of our country.
19. You may find bolas spiders near (your, you're) own home.
20. When (you're, your) looking for them, search in tall trees.
21. (Their, They're, There) will be no large web near the spider's home.
22. This spider doesn't wait for food to fly into (its, it's) web.
23. (It's, Its) interesting to watch a bolas catch (it's, its) food.
24. (It's, Its) like a cowhand (whose, who's) able to lasso a cow.
25. These spiders use (their, there) silk (to, too, two) lasso insects.
26. If the insects are (to, two, too) large, they break the lines of silk.
27. But often (they're, their, there) caught by the sticky strand.
28. Perhaps (your, you're) a person (who's, whose) afraid of spiders.
29. (Their, There) is no need (too, to, two) fear the bolas.
30. (Their, They're, There) not likely to harm people.

Adverbs That Modify Verbs

An *adverb* usually explains or describes a verb. It tells how, when, or where about the verb. It may stand before or after the verb, between the parts of the verb, or in another part of the sentence.

In each sentence draw a line under the adverb that modifies the italicized verb. On the line at the right of the sentence, write *how, when,* or *where* to show what the adverb tells about the verb. (Score: 2 for each sentence)

Example: Slowly he *walked* home.   _____*how*_____

Mountaineering

1. Early climbers often *gathered* scientific information.   _____

2. Later, mountaineering *became* a sport.   _____

3. Climbers *have* eagerly *climbed* the world's highest peaks.   _____

4. Recently, many difficult climbs *have been attempted*.   _____

5. A Japanese team of women bravely *scaled* Mt. Annapūrna III.   _____

6. A team of U.S. women successfully *climbed* Mt. McKinley.   _____

7. The southwest face of Mt. Everest *was* finally *climbed*.   _____

8. This climb *was* formerly *regarded* as impossible.   _____

9. Mountaineers always *climb* in groups.   _____

10. The climbers *move* upward with great care.   _____

11. Experienced climbers *handle* a rope expertly.   _____

12. They swiftly *descend* a mountain with a long rope.   _____

13. This technique *is* commonly *called* "rappelling."   _____

14. Climbing a snow-covered peak *can* often *be* dangerous.   _____

15. The weather conditions *are* changeable there.   _____

16. The sun sometimes *melts* the snow.   _____

17. The melted snow *may* then *turn* to ice.   _____

18. The climbers wisely *strap* spikes to their boots' soles.   _____

19. They carefully *make* their way up the mountain.   _____

20. Successful climbers *work* well as a team.   _____

Recognizing Adverbs

  26

Adverbs may explain or modify adjectives or other adverbs as well as verbs.

Draw a line under the adverb that modifies the italicized word or words.

Examples: The sun was <u>wonderfully</u> *warm*.

He ran <u>very</u> *quickly* to the house.

1. Ricardo Valdez has a very *interesting* job.
2. Paramedics *work* effectively as a team.
3. They *act* quickly in emergencies.
4. They skillfully *do* many things that doctors do.
5. Ricardo finds it extremely *rewarding* to help people.
6. Al Goldberg certainly *enjoys* his profession.
7. Al is a dietician in a fairly *large* hospital.
8. He carefully *plans* the menus for the hospital's patients.
9. He usually *suggests* a special diet for the patients.
10. Nancy Williams is extremely *interested* in computers.

11. She *is studying* thoroughly to be a computer programmer.
12. She *is* easily *learning* the computer languages.
13. Soon she will *use* the languages effectively.
14. Companies near Nancy's home definitely *need* programmers.
15. Jeffrey Jackson is an exceptionally *busy* administrator.
16. He works for a very *large* company as a personnel director.
17. All employees *will* probably *talk* with Jeffrey.
18. Jeffrey helps people find jobs that closely *match* their skills.
19. He cheerfully *answers* questions that people have.
20. He usually *helps train* the employees.
21. Jeffrey is wonderfully *talented* in helping people solve problems.

22. Fortunately, Lea Yamamoto *enjoys* the outdoors.
23. She *has* happily *worked* for the telephone company for five years.
24. Carefully Lea *repairs* lines that have fallen in bad weather.
25. She often *spends* four hours a day on top of a telephone pole!
26. Lea *does* her job well.
27. Carrie Sullivan is an exceptionally *good* photographer.
28. Daily, she *covers* sports for her city newspaper.
29. Carrie sometimes *attends* three games in one day!
30. Luckily, sports *are* her job.

More About Adverbs

 26

Draw one line under each adverb. Draw two lines under the word or words that the adverb explains or modifies.

Example: Some fish have a <u>very</u> <u>fine</u> sense of touch.

Animals and Their Senses

1. The senses of some animals are much keener than those of people.
2. Their senses are very important for their survival.
3. Some animals have an extremely keen sense of smell.
4. Dogs can often sense danger.
5. They can easily smell things from a great distance.
6. A dog certainly knows when its owner is coming.
7. It can tell by its extremely accurate sense of smell.
8. Fish are very dependent on their sense of smell.
9. Many fish would soon die without this sense.
10. Some animals have developed very sharp sight.
11. Hawks and vultures can see distinctly from great distances.
12. Owls can see well in the dark.
13. Other animals apparently have poor eyesight.
14. Dogs often are color-blind.
15. But some fish apparently can tell colors apart.
16. Other fish are quite blind.
17. Moles, which live under the ground, have very poor sight.
18. These nearly blind animals have developed their other senses.
19. They are extremely dependent on the senses of smell and hearing.
20. People usually say that a bat has poor sight.
21. But some bats do depend heavily on their vision.
22. They can always find their way at night.
23. Do bats have extremely sensitive hearing?
24. Some bats can hear very faint sounds.
25. These bats actually hear the sound of a small insect.
26. They will suddenly swerve to avoid the approach of an owl.
27. They hear the very swift movement of air from the owl's wings.
28. Do humans usually use these senses?
29. Humans, like other animals, often use their senses.
30. They also rely on their keen intelligence.

Better Speech   o— 26

I. Draw a line under the proper form in parentheses.

Example: You can see the moon (clear, <u>clearly</u>) tonight.

Telescopes

1. The heavens are (very, awful) interesting.
2. Centuries ago people (eager, eagerly) studied stars.
3. But they could not see the stars very (good, well).
4. Little was (actual, actually) known about the planets.
5. In 1609 a (very, real) great discovery was made.
6. An (exceptional, exceptionally) inventor built a telescope.
7. The planets must have seemed (somewhat, sort of) unreal.
8. The moon seemed (near, nearly) close enough to touch.
9. Large craters on the moon were seen (clearly, clear) for the first time.
10. People were (sure, surely) interested in the telescope.
11. Now they could see the stars and planets (good, well).

II. On the line write a word that is better than the italicized word or words in the sentence. If you can't think of a better word, write one that means the same thing or almost the same thing as the italicized word or words.

Example: Today's telescopes are *awfully* powerful.   _____*very*_____

12. Most telescopes are *really* huge.   _____

13. They are often *nearly* sixty feet long.   _____

14. People *commonly* use the refracting telescope.   _____

15. *Maybe* you have looked through a refracting telescope. _____

16. The glass lenses must be *rightly* made.   _____

17. These refracting telescopes are *conveniently* used.   _____

18. The reflecting telescope is *sort of* inconvenient to use. _____

19. *Oddly* enough, the viewer looks down this telescope.   _____

20. The viewer also sits *way up* in the air.   _____

21. The viewer *anxiously* looks down into a mirror.   _____

22. The *brilliantly* polished mirror reflects the sky.   _____

77

Adverbs and Adjectives

🔑 25, 26

I. Form adverbs from the following adjectives.

Examples: *gentle, gently   lazy, lazily   polite, politely*

1.	bitter	_____	12.	slight	_____
2.	curious	_____	13.	sharp	_____
3.	eager	_____	14.	exact	_____
4.	simple	_____	15.	fierce	_____
5.	most	_____	16.	heavy	_____
6.	angry	_____	17.	distant	_____
7.	clear	_____	18.	entire	_____
8.	proud	_____	19.	serious	_____
9.	sudden	_____	20.	late	_____
10.	wise	_____	21.	weary	_____
11.	even	_____	22.	sad	_____

II. Draw a line under the proper form in parentheses.

Health Protection

23. Diseases must be kept from spreading (wide, widely).
24. Communities work (persistent, persistently) to protect our health.
25. The city water supply is (frequent, frequently) tested for purity.
26. Chlorine gas kills disease germs in water (prompt, promptly).
27. Lime and alum cause (solid, solidly) dirt to settle to the bottom.
28. Filtration is a (common, commonly) method used to purify water.
29. The water filters (slow, slowly) through sand or charcoal.
30. Communities must do this job (good, well) to ensure pure water.
31. Garbage and sewage must be removed (safe, safely) and (regular, regularly).
32. Harmful germs grow and multiply (rapid, rapidly) in garbage and sewage.
33. Garbage cans should be kept covered (tight, tightly).
34. Places where food is handled are inspected (careful, carefully).
35. Streets must be cleaned often and (thorough, thoroughly).
36. Germs spread (quick, quickly) through the air over a (wide, widely) area.

Choosing Proper Forms

☞ 20, 23, 24, 25, 26, 36, 40

Draw a line under the proper form in parentheses.

Tools for Writing

1. It is hard to believe that once there weren't (no, any) books.
2. (No, Know) writing was (did, done) by early cave dwellers.
3. People couldn't (ever, never) write down the things they (knew, new).
4. People first (began, begun) to write with pictures.
5. Pictures (became, become) the symbols for words.
6. Egyptians had (began, begun) to write about three thousand years ago.
7. These people had (became, become) skillful at making paper.
8. Did you (know, no) that the paper was made from the papyrus plant?
9. This plant had (came, come) from the shores of the Nile River.
10. The Egyptians used an ink similar to (our, hour) own.
11. The papyrus was rolled up after the writing was (did, done).
12. Some of the books (was, were) over fifty feet long.
13. In other countries papyrus (wasn't, was) never used.
14. Some people had (began, begun) to write on soft clay tablets.
15. The tablets (became, become) hard when they were dried in the sun.
16. They were (to, too, two) hard (to, too, two) break easily.
17. A few centuries ago people (did, done) very little reading.
18. There were few people (which, who) could (buy, by) expensive books.
19. Scarcely (no, any) paper was made.
20. People (did, done) much writing on animal skins.
21. They copied (buy, by) hand their books, (who, which) (was, were) very valuable.
22. It took much more than (a, an) (our, hour) for a book to be copied.
23. Someone might spend a year or (too, two) making a (knew, new) copy of a book.
24. About five hundred years ago paper had (became, become) common.
25. More and more people (began, begun) to use paper for writing.
26. But there (weren't, were) no fountain pens or pencils.
27. Sometimes a feather, (who, which) had been sharpened, was used as a pen.
28. A feather (was, were) dipped in ink to (draw, drawn) the letters.
29. The printing press (came, come) into use early in the fifteenth century.
30. Books (became, become) more easily available.
31. Millions of books (are, is) now being printed each year.
32. Printing has (became, become) a very fast process.
33. Computers (is, are) used by most modern printers.

Word Division

🔑 42

Rewrite the words below, dividing them into syllables. If a word cannot be divided, place an *X* on the line next to the word.

Examples: waited _____*wait-ed*_____   rocked _____*X*_____

1.	loaded	_____	25.	daring	_____
2.	bumped	_____	26.	lemon	_____
3.	rained	_____	27.	blame	_____
4.	blotter	_____	28.	broken	_____
5.	wilted	_____	29.	subway	_____
6.	wished	_____	30.	missed	_____
7.	beaten	_____	31.	dishes	_____
8.	dance	_____	32.	cupful	_____
9.	fluffy	_____	33.	filled	_____
10.	thought	_____	34.	minded	_____
11.	gleamed	_____	35.	wider	_____
12.	actor	_____	36.	triangle	_____
13.	giant	_____	37.	overnight	_____
14.	printed	_____	38.	divided	_____
15.	here	_____	39.	helpless	_____
16.	hasty	_____	40.	helped	_____
17.	whiten	_____	41.	later	_____
18.	rancher	_____	42.	eaten	_____
19.	driver	_____	43.	parchment	_____
20.	healthful	_____	44.	northwestern	_____
21.	violet	_____	45.	motionless	_____
22.	compound	_____	46.	postpone	_____
23.	protect	_____	47.	tissue	_____
24.	legend	_____	48.	coconut	_____

Punctuation and Capitalization   ⚷ 1–11

Draw a line under each letter that should be
capitalized. Place punctuation marks where
they are needed.

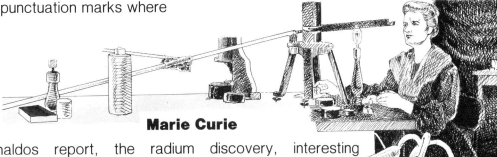

Marie Curie

1. Wasn't Renaldos report, the radium discovery, interesting

2. It tells about the work of marie curie.

3. Marie was born in poland on november 7 1867.

4. Her father, professor sklodowski, was a scientist.

5. Yes he taught Marie many interesting things about his work.

6. One day Marie said, "father ive decided that i want to be a scientist."

7. She went to paris, france, in the fall of 1891.

8. Marie wanted to study at the sorbonne.

9. There wasnt much money to spend for Maries education.

10. She lived in an attic room that was small cold and drafty.

11. One day she met Pierre Curie, a young french scientist.

12. In july 1895 Marie and Pierre were married.

13. Pierre's father, dr Eugene Curie, came to live with them.

14. Marie began to study a metal that was strange rare and fascinating.

15. Something in this metal gives off strange rays Pierre she said.

16. Perhaps i can learn what causes the rays she added.

17. Marie worked for hours in a laboratory that was cold damp and dark.

18. Finally, marie learned what caused the rays.

19. On december 26 1896 Marie announced her discovery.

20. Hadnt she discovered a new element called radium

21. Yes this rare element was Maries discovery.

22. She worked studied and experimented with radium for many years

23. Other european and american scientists also studied the element.

24. Many people were grateful for the exciting discovery

25. What amazing things radium can do they said.

26. But how difficult it was to find this rare expensive element

27. Wasnt Marie given a gift when she visited the united states

28. Yes american women gave her radium worth a hundred thousand dollars.

29. Marie used the gift for her work in paris

Punctuating a Friendly Letter   52, 54

I. Place punctuation marks where they are needed in the following letter. Draw a line under each word that should begin with a capital letter. (Score: 20)

7536 jackson road

los angeles california 90012

march 2 2007

dear sharon

    i am planning to have a party a week from next saturday Can you come and spend the weekend let me know where and when to meet you if you can come

your cousin

kay

II. On the lines below write a letter accepting an invitation to spend the weekend with a friend. Use your own address and today's date. (Score: 30)

_____

_____

_____

_____

_____

_____

_____

_____

_____

_____

_____

_____

_____

Other Things to Do: Write a letter to one of your relatives, telling about your recent activities. Check your letter carefully. Then mail it.

Writing a Business Letter   ⌐ 52, 55

On the lines below write a letter in answer to one of the following advertisements. Use your own address and today's date in the heading. (Score: 30)

Beach Balls, $5

3 feet high. Fun for the whole family. Inflates easily. Guaranteed not to burst or break. Send check, cash, or money order to: Stein Rubber Products, 3705 Oak Drive, Detroit, Michigan 48218.

Fun for All!

Get your new Hobby Catalogue, which lists tools, supplies, and suggestions for working with leather, metal, wood, plastic, and clay. Send to: J. L. Jammer Company, 389 Main Street, Boston, Massachusetts 02190.

Remembering What We Have Learned

1. Write two sentences to describe yourself. Draw one line under each adjective you use. 🔑 25

_____

_____

2. Write two sentences about your favorite sport. Use an adverb in each sentence. 🔑 26

_____

_____

3. Write two three-syllable words on the following lines. Place hyphens between the syllables. 🔑 42

_____   _____

4. Write the possessive forms of two nouns. 🔑 15

_____   _____

5. Write a short business letter, ordering a record catalog from a music store. 🔑 52, 55

_____

_____

_____

_____

_____

_____

_____

_____

6. On each line below write a sentence, using one of the words in parentheses at the left of the line. 🔑 25, 26

(a, an) _____

(good, well) _____

Writing Descriptions

🔑 25, 26

The skillful use of adjectives and adverbs helps to make descriptions clear and precise. Be careful not to overload your describing sentences; tell only what is necessary to make your description effective. Decide which sentence in the examples is the most effective description of a stormy sky.

Examples: It was a cloudy day.

On Monday the sky was dark and cloudy.

The troubled sky was the color of putty.

I.   Write a descriptive sentence about each subject listed below. (Score: 25)

1.   (A sour pickle) _____

_____

2.   (A burning candle) _____

_____

3.   (Popcorn) _____

_____

4.   (An icicle) _____

_____

5.   (A cricket) _____

_____

II.   Write a paragraph describing how you look, act, and feel when you get out of bed in the morning. (Score: 25)

_____

_____

_____

_____

_____

_____

_____

_____

Sentence Elements

 45

On the lines below write the complete subject and the complete predicate of the following sentences. (Score: 2 for each subject and 2 for each predicate)

About Comets

1. Many people once greatly feared comets.
2. We are no longer afraid of them.
3. Scientists have studied them for centuries.
4. Some comets look like stars with tails.
5. The tail may be millions of kilometers long.
6. Other comets seem to be cloudy spots of light.
7. We can see only a few comets with the naked eye.
8. Most comets must be seen through a telescope.
9. A famous comet was seen in 1910 and in 1986.
10. It was named for the astronomer Edmund Halley.
11. Your parents may have seen Halley's comet in 1986.
12. It will probably be seen again in 2062, a 76-year orbit.

Complete Subject   *Complete Predicate*

1._____   _____

2._____   _____

3._____   _____

4._____   _____

5._____   _____

6._____   _____

7._____   _____

8._____   _____

9._____   _____

10._____   _____

11._____   _____

12._____   _____

Other Things to Do: Write five sentences about the sun, the moon, the planets, or the stars. Draw one line under each adjective and two lines under each adverb in your sentences.

Reviewing Simple Subject and Predicate    45

Draw a line under the noun or pronoun used
as the simple subject. Draw two lines under
the verb or verb phrase that is the simple
predicate. (Score: 1 for each subject and 1
for each predicate)

Example: <u>Anna Paphas</u> <u><u>entered</u></u> our

class this fall.

A Student From Greece

1. We asked Anna many questions about her country.

2. She told us about the city of Corinth.

3. Did you go to school in Corinth?

4. Yes, I went to a grade school there.

5. My parents had a business in Corinth.

6. They exported currants and figs to other countries.

7. How do people dress in your country?

8. City residents dress much like Americans.

9. But for special celebrations people may wear native costumes.

10. The men sometimes wear short, full skirts.

11. Braided jackets complete their costumes.

12. The women's costume is a blouse and a long, brightly colored skirt.

13. Materials for the costumes are woven by the people.

14. Was Corinth a famous city of ancient Greece?

15. Yes, it had been known for centuries as a trading center.

16. Ships from many countries filled its harbors.

17. In 1858 Corinth was destroyed by an earthquake.

18. Later a new city was built near the ruins.

19. Today Corinth is considered a very modern city.

20. Visitors to Corinth can still visit the ruins of the ancient city.

21. Anna will make an exhibit on Greek life for our classroom.

22. She has many slides of Athens and Corinth.

23. Anna may bring her native costume.

24. She promised to teach us a native dance.

25. We hope she brings samples of delicious Greek food!

Recognizing Prepositions

🔑 27 a

A preposition is always followed by a noun or a pronoun. Other words are sometimes used between the preposition and the noun or pronoun following it.

In the blank opposite each sentence write the preposition that connects the italicized word or words to the rest of the sentence.

Example: The boat sailed toward the *statue*.   *toward*
_____

The Statue of Liberty

1.   The statue stands on *Liberty Island* in New York Harbor.   _____

2.   The name of the *statue* is Liberty Enlightening the World.   _____

3.   France gave the statue to the *United States* in 1884.   _____

4.   It symbolizes liberty under a free *form* of government.   _____

5.   Visitors come between the *months* of May and October.   _____

6.   Ships can see the figure clearly during the *day*.   _____

7.   The statue is illuminated throughout the *night*.   _____

8.   Floodlights shine from the *base* of the statue.   _____

9.   The statue represents a woman dressed in a long *robe*.   _____

10.   The woman is holding a torch above her *head*.   _____

11.   She grasps a tablet with her left *hand*.   _____

12.   Engraved upon the *tablet* is the date July 4, 1776.   _____

13.   The statue was designed by *Frédéric-Auguste Bartholde*.   _____

14.   It is made of copper sheets hammered into *shape* by hand.   _____

15.   The pieces were assembled over a steel *framework*.   _____

16.   The torch of the statue shines through leaded *glass*.   _____

17.   Steps inside the *statue* lead from the base to the head.   _____

18.   At the *base* of the statue is a museum.   _____

19.   People come from around the *world* to see the statue.   _____

20.   It stands 92 meters (305 feet) high with its *pedestal*.   _____

21.   The statue can be seen by *all* who visit the harbor.   _____

Prepositional Phrases

27 b, c, d

When prepositional phrases explain or modify verbs, they tell how, when, or where. When prepositional phrases explain or modify nouns or pronouns, they tell which one or what kind.

I.   On the line write the verb or verb phrase that the italicized prepositional phrase modifies.

Example: I read about an astronomer *in the library* today.   _____ *read* _____

Astronomer, Henrietta Leavitt

1.   Henrietta Leavitt was born *in Massachusetts*.   _____

2.   She studied *at the Harvard College Observatory*.   _____

3.   She studied special stars *for many years*.   _____

4.   Little was known about them *before her studies*.   _____

5.   These stars seemed brighter *at certain times*.   _____

6.   *For a few days*, a star would shine brightly.   _____

7.   *After a while*, it would fade.   _____

8.   Some stars remained bright *for several months*.   _____

9.   She studied these stars *with great interest*.   _____

II.   On the line write the noun that the italicized prepositional phrase modifies.

10.   Henrietta Leavitt had a new theory *about these stars*.   _____

11.   She conducted many studies *of star brightness*.   _____

12.   She developed a system *for measuring* star brightness.   _____

13.   The brightness *of many stars* was then compared.   _____

14.   She also made several discoveries *of new stars*.   _____

15.   The discovery *of four novas* was among these.   _____

16.   Ms. Leavitt was an important contributor *to modern science*.   _____

17.   Her studies laid the groundwork *for later discoveries*.   _____

18.   Astronomers *of the future* will benefit from her work.   _____

Other Things to Do: Draw a circle around each italicized preposition above.

Prepositional Phrases

 27

The noun or pronoun that goes with a preposition may be separated from the preposition by one or more adjectives. Two or more nouns or pronouns may go with one preposition.

In the sentences below place parentheses around each complete prepositional phrase (there may be more than one in the sentence). Draw a line under the nouns or pronouns that go with the preposition.

Example: You have probably seen stained glass (at some time).

Stained-Glass Windows

1. The art of making stained-glass windows is a very old one.

2. Not much is known about the origin of the art.

3. It may have begun in Egypt.

4. It spread to Europe in the ninth century.

5. Venice, Italy, was an early center for the arts.

6. The oldest stained-glass windows still in existence may be found in Germany.

7. The early windows were made by a rather simple technique.

8. First a pattern for the window was drawn by an artist.

9. Then pieces of glass were colored by a chemical method or process.

10. They were placed on a table and cut to the pattern.

11. Strips of soft lead were placed between them.

12. When the lead hardened, it held the glass in place.

13. Then the glass was placed in the arch of a church window.

14. Usually the early windows told the stories of religious figures.

15. Today they may be used for any topic.

16. This fine art was almost lost in the eighteenth and nineteenth centuries.

17. One day a little boy and his father visited Notre Dame Cathedral in Paris.

18. He saw the lovely windows and heard the tones of the beautiful organ.

19. He cried to his father, "The windows are singing!"

20. When the boy was grown, he became a master architect in Europe.

21. He wrote a famous book about architecture and stained-glass windows.

22. We owe to him and his book the revival of interest in the art.

Using Prepositions

🔑 27 e, 34, 35

I. Draw a line under the proper form in parentheses.

Example: I walked (between, among) Gary and Flo to the animal park.

The Wild Animal Park

1.   Gary, Flo, and I went (in, into) the animal park.

2.   (Inside, Inside of) the park were large fenced areas.

3.   There were people waiting (in, into) line to get (in, into) a train.

4.   The train took the visitors (in, into) the various fenced areas.

5.   There were wild cats (in, into) the first area.

6.   A lion cub sat (between, among) two lions.

7.   At one end (of, off) the fenced area was the lions' den.

8.   A lion was standing (outside, outside of) the den.

9.   (Between, Among) the many lions were wild birds.

10.   The train took us (into, in) the next large area.

11.   We saw a hippopotamus sliding (in, into) a pond.

12.   The natural smells of the wild were coming (from, off) the pond.

13.   A tour guide told us about the animals as we rode (between, among) them.

14.   "The purpose (of, off) this park is to preserve the animals' environment," she said.

15.   People are kept (off, off of) the animals' land.

II.   Draw a line under the proper expression in parentheses.

16.   Do you see (them, those) baby giraffes on the left?

17.   We (knew, knowed) that they would only survive in their natural habitat.

18.   Gary (drew, drawed) a sketch of the giraffe while the guide continued.

19.   "It (ain't, isn't) easy to maintain a safe environment for them," she said.

20.   A hippopotamus (dragged, drug) itself from the pond as she spoke.

21.   We (heard, heared) her explain how the park feeds the animals.

22.   Many animals (et, ate) food that was naturally found in their fenced area.

23.   "A (grown, growed) giraffe will eat the natural vegetation," she explained.

24.   "The animals take care of (themselves, theirselves) when possible," she said.

25.   If you look closely, you will see a lion that was (born, borned) last month.

26.   The cub probably (couldn't have, couldn't of) been born in a zoo.

27.   "The cub and its mother are near (those, them) rocks now," she said.

28.   As we left the park, we (bought, buyed) postcards to send to friends.

29.   We (couldn't have, couldn't of) had a better day.

Recognizing Interjections

○━ 24, 29, 35, 40

An *interjection* is a word that expresses strong or sudden feeling.

I.   Draw a line under each interjection in the sentences below.

Example: Oh! I've found the treasure!

1.   Hurry! We'll miss the train!
2.   Oh! What's the matter?
3.   Look! There are the northern lights.
4.   Hurrah! He hit a home run!
5.   Ah! This ice cream is good.
6.   Hello! We're glad to see you.
7.   Indeed! That's an odd idea.
8.   Quick! Hand me the wrench.
9.   Whew! That was an exciting play.
10.   Well! Where have you been?
11.   Nonsense! He can't mean what he's saying.
12.   Aha! I found the answer.
13.   Good! I'm glad you found it.
14.   Hi! I'm happy to see you again.
15.   Hush! The curtain is rising.

II.   Draw a line under the proper form in parentheses.

16.   Ginny has (build, built) a model hot air balloon.
17.   She (bringed, brought) the model (too, to, two) school.
18.   She had (buyed, bought) the model kit at a hobby shop.
19.   She showed us how a balloon is (drove, driven) through the air by wind.
20.   The (great, grate) balloon may be (maked, made) of silk or plastic.
21.   Ginny also (spoke, spoken) about helium, a type of gas used in balloons.
22.   The helium makes the balloon (raise, rise).
23.   When we (swam, swum) in the (sea, see), we lay on inflated rubber rafts.
24.   Ginny (sayed, said) that the balloon floats in air in much the same way.
25.   We had (thinked, thought) that balloons were used mainly in circuses.
26.   But Ginny told us that (they're, there) also used for scientific purposes.
27.   Hot air balloons are often (flown, flied) for sport and recreation.
28.   Balloonists who have risen high in the air have (wore, worn) special suits.
29.   (They're, Their) helping scientists (to, too, two) learn about weather.
30.   Would you like to (ride, ridden) in a hot air balloon?

Conjunctions

28 a, b

A *conjunction* may connect single words, groups of words, or groups of ideas.

Draw a line under each conjunction in the following sentences.

Examples: I enjoy church bells <u>and</u> chimes.

Bells have a lovely tone, <u>and</u> the sound carries for great distances.

<u>When</u> George visited Europe, he heard many kinds of bells.

Bells and Their Uses

1.   Bells are an important and useful part of our everyday lives.
2.   We arise when the alarm clock rings.
3.   We attend classes and schedule school activities by bells.
4.   Bells are used in factories to tell the workers when they are to stop work.
5.   When Sunday comes, we often hear church bells ringing.
6.   Bells are also used on riverboats and seagoing ships.
7.   There they mark the hours and sound alarms.
8.   Bells on buoys at sea mark dangerous channels or coastlines.
9.   When mealtime comes on the farm, a bell calls workers from the fields.
10.   Long ago, when communication was difficult, bells were rung in emergencies.
11.   Because they could be heard far away, they were used as signals.
12.   In many European countries bells are rung for weddings, funerals, and births.
13.   Bells may announce the arrival of either a ship or an important visitor.
14.   One famous bell is a symbol of freedom and independence.
15.   Church bells are molded from copper and tin.
16.   The mold is made of iron and baked clay.
17.   When the mold is ready, hot, liquid metal is poured into it.
18.   The metal must cool slowly, for rapid cooling will cause it to break.
19.   Neither time nor frequent use will destroy a bell if it is properly made.
20.   Bells are made in several sizes, weights, and thicknesses.
21.   Size and thickness are important, since they determine the tone of the bell.
22.   I have read that in Burma there is a bell weighing eighty tons.
23.   It is said that bells were first used in China thousands of years ago.
24.   They were introduced into France about 550 and into England a century later.
25.   As bells became more popular, bell towers were built.
26.   The Leaning Tower of Pisa and the Singing Tower in Florida are bell towers.

Avoiding Too Many *And*s   ⟰ 28 d

The sentences in the paragraphs below contain too many *and*s. Rewrite the paragraphs, using shorter, clearer sentences. (Score: 2 for each correct sentence)

An Aquarium

Heidi and Carey built an aquarium and the frame is made of metal and the sides and bottom are glass and Heidi brought sand from the riverbank to place on the bottom of the tank and she and Carey placed the tank near a large window and filled it with water and then they went to the pet shop and bought several water plants and some tropical fish and all their friends enjoy watching the tiny, beautiful fish.

_____

_____

_____

_____

_____

_____

A Visit to an Oceanarium

When they were in St. Augustine, Florida, Mr. Williams took David and Mindy to an oceanarium and an oceanarium is a huge steel and concrete aquarium that is built near the ocean and it is filled with sea water so that salt-water fish can live in it and there are large windows in the aquarium, where people can watch the fish and David and Mindy took several pictures of the fish through the windows.

_____

_____

_____

_____

_____

_____

_____

Compound Subjects and Predicates

🔑 45 d, e

The subject of a sentence may be *compound*—**that is, it may have two or more parts. A predicate may also be compound. Both subject and predicate may be compound.**

Examples: *Marco Polo* and his *family* lived in the thirteenth century.

Marco *traveled* and *explored* in many little-known countries.

Marco and his *family lived* in Venice and *worked* as traders.

Draw one line under the compound simple subjects and two lines under the compound simple predicates.

A Medieval Traveler

1.   Nicolo Polo and Maffeo Polo were Marco's father and uncle.

2.   Marco's father and uncle first went to the Orient alone as traders.

3.   There they sold their goods and visited the country of Cathay.

4.   Cathay and China are two names for the same country.

5.   They were received and were made welcome by Kublai Khan, the Chinese ruler.

6.   Kublai Khan and his court had never seen Europeans before.

7.   He asked them questions and learned much about Europe.

8.   Some time later Nicolo and Maffeo decided to return to Venice.

9.   Transportation and communication were very slow in those days.

10.   The Polos traveled for two years and finally arrived in Italy.

11.   A few years later Nicolo and Maffeo left again for the Orient.

12.   Marco, Nicolo's son, had grown up and was now a young man of seventeen.

13.   Marco's father and uncle decided to take Marco to Cathay with them.

14.   Finally the weary travelers reached Cathay and found the Emperor.

15.   Kublai Khan liked Marco and made him an attendant at court.

16.   Marco and the Khan quickly became close friends.

17.   The Khan appointed Marco to high office and made him governor of Yangchow.

18.   Marco left the court and journeyed to the city of Yangchow.

19.   On the way he observed the people and noted their way of life.

20.   Marco admired and respected the culture of the Chinese.

21.   Kublai and other Oriental rulers of the time were concerned about their people.

22.   For many years Marco traveled and explored the Orient for the Khan.

23.   Finally he and his family left Cathay and journeyed home to Venice.

24.   At first no one in Venice recognized or welcomed them.

25.   Marco's strange tales of the Orient were read widely but were not believed.

26.   Centuries later, explorers and travelers visited China and verified his tales.

Unnecessary Words

 34

Draw a line through all the unnecessary words in the following sentences. (Score: 1 for each word or group of words correctly crossed out)

The Tale of the Emperor

1.   Once an Emperor he cared only for the finest clothes.
2.   He went and rode through the streets so that everyone could see his clothes.
3.   One day two unknown men came inside of the city gates.
4.   The men they said that they could weave the most wonderful cloth.
5.   The cloth it couldn't be seen by people who were unfit for their jobs.
6.   The Emperor he wanted to have some of this here cloth.
7.   The Emperor went and had the weavers brought to him at once.
8.   Then the Emperor he gave them a huge sum of money to begin their work.
9.   Quickly the weavers they set up two large looms.
10.   They had got the finest silk thread sent to the palace.
11.   The weavers then put this here thread into their own pockets.
12.   They went and pretended to work at the empty looms all day and night.
13.   The Emperor he could hear the rattling of the looms.
14.   The news of the magical cloth it spread throughout the city.
15.   The Emperor sent his trusted Minister to inspect there the weavers' work.
16.   He knew that his faithful Minister he could see the cloth.
17.   But when the Minister arrived, he couldn't see where the cloth was at.
18.   Because the weavers praised the cloth, the Minister he said nothing.
19.   He returned back to the palace with the news that the cloth was beautiful.
20.   This here was the day for the Emperor to wear his new clothes.
21.   The people followed him when they saw where he was going to.
22.   Imagine his surprise when he went and saw the looms!
23.   The Emperor he complimented the weavers on the lovely clothes.
24.   They pretended to take the cloth off of the looms.
25.   They asked the Emperor to try on this here new cloak.
26.   They pretended to cover over the Emperor with the cloak.
27.   The Emperor marched in the parade as the people they watched.
28.   The Emperor he proudly held up his head.
29.   No one dared mention the Emperor's here condition.
30.   Everyone they pretended to see the new clothes.
31.   Then a child said, "But the Emperor he has no clothes!"
32.   As the Emperor marched, he knew that this here child spoke the truth.

Using *Sit* and *Set, Lie* and *Lay*   ⚷ 32, 33

To *sit* means to be seated. To *set* means to place or put something.

To *lie* means to rest or recline. To *lay* means to place or put something.

Examples: Kim has *sat* down on the train.   She *set* her suitcase in the aisle.

Tonight she will *lie* in a berth.   She *laid* her ticket in her suitcase.

Draw a line under the proper form in parentheses.

Trains of Yesterday and Today

1.   Kim, please (lie, lay) your jacket on the back of the chair.

2.   You may (sit, set) your luggage in the overhead rack.

3.   Would you like to (sit, set) by the window?

4.   The first American trains were (sat, set) in motion about 1800.

5.   Early trains in which passengers (sat, set) were horse-drawn coaches on rails.

6.   The first railroad rails that were (lain, laid) were made of wood.

7.   The rails sometimes (lay, laid) over stone crossties.

8.   Modern steel rails are (sit, set) upon wooden crossties.

9.   The rails have been (sat, set) over the ties and fastened with steel spikes.

10.   Modern tracks are (lain, laid) down with a special machine.

11.   This machine can (lie, lay) about two miles of track a day.

12.   The tracks (lie, lay) over a roadbed made up of crushed rock.

13.   Some railroads have (lain, laid) parallel sets of tracks.

14.   Two trains can then (sit, set) on the tracks and move in opposite directions.

15.   If there is only one set of tracks, one train must (sit, set) on a siding.

16.   It (sits, sets) there and waits until the other train has gone by.

17.   Railroad tracks are (lain, laid) on a level, straight roadbed when possible.

18.   A level roadbed is more comfortable for the people who (sit, set) on the train.

19.   The train we have (sat, set) in is very restful.

20.   Tonight when we (lie, lay) in our berths, we shall sleep comfortably.

21.   The first sleeping cars had hard bunks on which the passengers (lay, laid).

22.   All day the travelers had (sat, set) in drafty coaches lit by candles.

23.   Passengers who had (sat, set) down by a window might get a cinder in their eyes.

24.   Today's traveler (sits, sets) in an elegant passenger car.

25.   Passengers might (lay, lie) back in their seats as they would in an airplane.

26.   Food might be (sat, set) on a tray in front of their seats.

27.   Train travelers (sit, set) for less time on today's fast trains.

Choosing Proper Forms

Draw a line under the proper form in parentheses.

Bicycling

1. Bicycles (is, are) used for transportation in many countries.
2. (They, Them) are also used for sport.
3. Some people have ridden long distances (by, buy) bicycle.
4. Cycling (has, have) become a popular sport in the United States.
5. (A, An) bicycle is economical and efficient.
6. Riding can also (be, bee) a lot of fun!
7. (Is, Are) there many kinds of bicycles?
8. Some bicycles are (build, built) for touring.
9. They are sturdy and can be (rode, ridden) long distances.
10. Other bicycles are (made, maid) especially for racing.
11. (They, Them) are very lightweight and have special equipment.
12. Have you (heard, heared) of the Tour de France?
13. Cyclists from many countries come (to, too) France for this race.
14. The Tour (it is, is) extremely long and hard.
15. It has (taken, took) riders up and down the Alps.
16. (Its, It's) a very difficult race to finish and takes many days.
17. The racers eat and (drink, drank) while on their bikes.
18. They (wear, worn) helmets and very lightweight clothing.
19. The (great, grate) riders of the world compete for the winning trophy.
20. Winners of this race have (risen, rised) to world fame.
21. You (may have, may of) seen track riders in the Olympic games.
22. (Won, One) of the finest tracks in the world is in Trexlertown, Pennsylvania.
23. Track riders specialize (in, into) riding fast for short distances.
24. They (don't, doesn't) usually ride long distances.
25. The oval cycling tracks (has, have) sloping sides.
26. (This, This here) helps the riders stay upright when riding fast.
27. But they must be careful not to (fell, fall) when riding slowly!
28. Expert riders use (a, an) technique called "drafting."
29. A rider (who, that) drafts is pulled by the suction, or draft, of the rider ahead.
30. This helps a racer (save, save on) energy until the last minute!
31. Racers work together until (they, them) pull away from the "pack."
32. Then there (is, are) a fast sprint to the finish.
33. Have you (rode, ridden) a bicycle lately?

Outlining a Story

47

Study the picture below. Then read the main headings in the outline below, and invent a fanciful story based on the picture. Fill in the subtopics in the outline. (Score: 2 for each subtopic)

A Space Flight

I. Departure from Earth

    A. _____

    B. _____

    C. _____

II. Traveling through space

    A. _____

    B. _____

    C. _____

III. Landing on the planet Xenon

    A. _____

    B. _____

    C. _____

IV. Departure from Xenon

    A. _____

    B. _____

    C. _____

Other Things to Do: On a separate sheet of paper write the story you have outlined.

Remembering What We Have Learned

1.   Write two sentences, using a compound simple subject and a compound simple predicate in each. ⚷ 45 d, e

_____

_____

2.   Write three sentences. Use a preposition in the first sentence, a conjunction in the second, and an interjection in the third. ⚷ 27, 28, 29

_____

_____

_____

3.   Write two sentences. In the first sentence use a prepositional phrase that modifies a noun, and in the second use a prepositional phrase that modifies a verb. ⚷ 27 b, c, d

_____

_____

_____

4.   Write a short paragraph about a myth or legend you have heard. Use two conjunctions other than _and._ ⚷ 28 c, d

_____

_____

_____

_____

5.   On each line below write a sentence, using one of the words in parentheses at the left of the line. ⚷ 27 e, 32, 33

(between, among) _____

(in, into) _____

(off, from) _____

(sit, set) _____

(lie, lay) _____

Parts of Speech

🔑 13, 16, 21, 25, 26, 27, 28, 29

In these sentences write the part of speech above each underlined word. Use the following abbreviations: *n.* (noun); *pron.* (pronoun); *v.* (verb); *adv.* (adverb); *adj.* (adjective); *prep.* (preposition); *conj.* (conjunction); *interj.* (interjection).

                       pron.   adv. prep.   n.

Example: Have you ever looked closely at a dollar bill?

About the Great Seal

1. Dollar bills are sometimes called greenbacks.

2. If you look at the green side of a bill, you will see a seal.

3. The front and the back sides of the seal are shown.

4. This is the Great Seal of the United States.

5. This important seal must be used on all official papers.

6. You will always find the Great Seal on all laws.

7. They have clearly seen the eagle on the face side of the Great Seal.

8. Here in the claws of the left foot is a sheaf of arrows.

9. He showed me the olive branch held by the claws of the right foot.

10. She says that the arrows mean that we must defend our country.

11. John told us that the olive branch symbolizes peace.

12. The thirteen stars must surely stand for the thirteen original states.

13. Then Sharon said that the shield represents self-reliance.

14. Oh! I see a pyramid on the back of the seal.

15. This solid pyramid signifies the strength and endurance of the United States.

16. Across the base of the pyramid is written the date 1776.

17. The Continental Congress adopted our Declaration of Independence on July 4, 1776.

Other Things to Do: Use reference books to learn all you can about the flag of the United States. Find out what the colors, the stars, and the stripes stand for. Then write a composition about the meaning of our flag.

Choosing Proper Forms

🔑 23, 24, 32

Draw a line under the proper word in parentheses in each of the following sentences. (Score: 1 for each word correctly underlined)

Example: There (is, <u>are</u>) boats on the lake.

Sailing

1. (Doesn't, Don't) the sight of graceful sailboats excite you?
2. The boat you (saw, seen) coming toward the dock is a catboat.
3. Catboats (is, are) the simplest kind of sailboats.
4. They (was, were) (gave, given) their name because they have cat rigs.
5. Cat rigs (has, have) only one mast, which is (set, sat) toward the front of the boat.
6. (Is, Are) there two sails fastened to the mast of a catboat?
7. No, only one sail is (ran, run) up the mast.
8. But sometimes a small flag is (flew, flown) from the top of the mast.
9. Have you (went, gone) close enough to the mast to see how the sail is fastened?
10. Sometimes bronze fittings (fastens, fasten) the sail to the mast.
11. The sail is (drew, drawn) up and down by ropes called "halyards."
12. It is spread out at the bottom by being (ran, run) along a pole called the "boom."
13. (Doesn't, Don't) a wide board run along the bottom of a catboat?
14. Yes, this "centerboard" may be (drew, drawn) up or down.
15. The centerboard keeps the boat from being (blew, blown) in the wrong direction.
16. Rita (saw, seen) a catboat that had just (came, come) across the lake.
17. As the boat (drew, drawn) near, she saw that two friends (was, were) aboard.
18. Rita had never (rode, ridden) in a sailboat, so she (stole, stolen) a bit nearer.
19. The girls in the boat (spoke, spoken) to Rita and invited her aboard.
20. Rita asked the girls why the boat had (wove, woven) back and forth across the lake.
21. "The wind (blew, blown) from this direction today," the girls said.
22. The boat would be (threw, thrown) off its course if it sailed against the wind.
23. To travel against the wind, the boat (wove, woven) back and forth across the lake.
24. When a boat has (went, gone) in such a zig-zag course, it has been "tacking."
25. Later her friends (took, taken) Rita for a ride in the boat.
26. The sail was raised, and the wind (tore, torn) at it.
27. Rita soon (grew, grown) to like sailing.

Working With Verbs

🔑 23, 24

I. Write the missing principal parts of the verbs listed below.

	Present	*Past*	*Past Participle*
1.		drew	
2.			flown
3.	give		
4.			gone
5.		grew	
6.			seen
7.	tear		
8.		threw	
9.	steal		
10.			run

II. Draw a line under the proper form in parentheses.

11. Diamonds (is, are) one of the hardest minerals known on earth.

12. Diamonds (has, have) been found in many parts of the world.

13. The first diamond (was, were) found over 2,500 years ago in India.

14. Today the main source of diamonds (is, are) South Africa.

15. (Doesn't, Don't) most diamonds now come from Kimberley, South Africa?

16. Because they are such hard gems, diamonds (has, have) great value.

17. (Isn't, Aren't) diamonds used in industrial tools and for record needles?

18. Rough diamonds (is, are) found in many shapes and sizes.

19. Usually a rough diamond (is, are) dull.

20. (Isn't, Aren't) diamond dust used in cutting a diamond?

21. No other substance (cut, cuts) this hard gem.

22. After it (has, have) been cut and polished, the diamond has many brilliant sides.

23. Many men and women (like, likes) to wear diamonds.

24. (Wasn't, Weren't) the world's largest diamond the Cullinan diamond?

25. People (was, were) amazed at the size of this stone.

26. The diamond (was, were) one and one-third pounds in weight.

Singular and Plural Nouns

🔑 14

Study Key 14 until you understand the various ways to form plurals of singular nouns. Then form the plurals of the following nouns by observing the examples given.

Examples: donkey _____*donkeys*_____   pony   _____*ponies*_____

1. holiday _____   19. factory _____
2. toy _____   20. country _____
3. valley _____   21. baby _____
4. bay _____   22. city _____
5. monkey _____   23. fly _____
6. boy _____   24. puppy _____

Examples: loaf _____*loaves*_____   stereo   _____*stereos*_____

7. half _____   25. studio _____
8. knife _____   26. radio _____
9. thief _____   27. trio _____
10. life _____   28. rodeo _____

Examples: church _____*churches*_____   domino   _____*dominoes*_____

11. lunch _____   29. tomato _____
12. wish _____   30. echo _____
13. glass _____   31. potato _____
14. box _____   32. hero _____
15. watch _____   33. mosquito _____

Examples: chief _____*chiefs*_____   avocado   _____*avocados*_____

16. roof _____   34. solo _____
17. safe _____   35. piano _____
18. cliff _____   36. pueblo _____

Adjectives and Adverbs

25 a, 26

Draw a line under the proper form in parentheses.

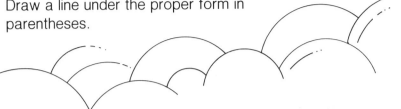

1. Apollo was the (greatly, great) sun god of the Greeks.
2. Each day he drove his (bright, brightly) sun chariot across the sky.
3. The (bright, brightly) shining chariot was drawn by strong horses.
4. Apollo (greatly, great) loved his son, Phaethon.
5. But one day Apollo made a (foolish, foolishly) promise to the boy.
6. He said that he would (glad, gladly) grant any wish to his son.
7. Phaethon (foolish, foolishly) asked to drive the sun chariot.
8. Apollo (anxiously, anxious) asked his son to change his mind.
9. The trip across the sky was (dangerous, dangerously) difficult.
10. But Phaethon was (eagerly, eager) to drive the great chariot.
11. He was sure that he could make the (dangerously, dangerous) trip.
12. Apollo (reluctantly, reluctant) kept his promise.
13. Phaethon was (glad, gladly) for a chance to drive the chariot.
14. The horses were (quick, quickly) harnessed to the chariot.
15. Everything was (final, finally) ready for the trip to begin.
16. The (reluctant, reluctantly) father gave the reins to his son.
17. Then Apollo gave his son some (final, finally) advice.
18. He told Phaethon to hold the reins (tight, tightly).
19. The (quick, quickly) horses sprang up into the sky.
20. But they did not feel Apollo's (firm, firmly) grip on the reins.
21. Soon they were running (wildly, wild) across the sky.
22. The chariot would sometimes come (terrible, terribly) close to the earth.
23. Then the (wild, wildly) horses would fly into the sky.
24. The chariot set (terribly, terrible) fires on the earth.
25. Everyone thought that the earth would (sure, surely) be destroyed.
26. Zeus, the ruling god, was (sure, surely) about what had to be done.
27. He must act (swift, swiftly) to stop the chariot.
28. Zeus (carefully, careful) prepared a thunderbolt.
29. He took (careful, carefully) aim at the sun chariot.
30. The (swiftly, swift) thunderbolt struck Phaethon from the chariot.

Prepositional Phrases

In each of these sentences there is a prepositional phrase in parentheses, and the word it modifies appears in italics. On the line at the right of the sentence tell whether the prepositional phrase is used as an adjective or an adverb. Use the abbreviations *adj.* and *adv.* (Score: 2 for each correct answer)

Examples: In a *lump* (of coal) there seems to be magic.   *adj.*

                 Many things *are made* (from coal).   *adv.*

Coal

1.   Have you ever *looked* closely (at coal)?   _____

2.   Let's look at a *piece* (of it).   _____

3.   *Look* (through a microscope) at it.   _____

4.   You may see the *print* (of a leaf) on the coal.   _____

5.   Coal *was formed* (from plants) long ago.   _____

6.   The plants *grew* (in large swamps).   _____

7.   The *plants* (of the swamp) died and fell.   _____

8.   Mud and sand *washed* (over the fallen plants).   _____

9.   (For many centuries) they *were buried.*   _____

10.   *Pressure* (on the plants) changed them.   _____

11.   They *were* slowly *changed* (to coal).   _____

12.   People first *used* coal (for fuel).   _____

13.   Today many things *are made* (from coal).   _____

14.   The *products* (of coal) are used every day.   _____

15.   We enjoy the *music* (on records).   _____

16.   Records are among the *products* (of coal).   _____

17.   The *nylon* (in this dress) came from coal.   _____

18.   Many perfumes *began* (with a lump) of coal.   _____

19.   Detergent *is made* (for us) from this mineral.   _____

20.   Coal *is found* (in deep mines).   _____

21.   This resource is *important* (to us).   _____

Reviewing Sentence Recognition   ⊶ 6, 7, 8, 45 a

I. Write *No* after the groups of words below that are not sentences. Write *Yes* after the groups of words that are sentences. (Score: 10)

The Traveling Eel

1. The freshwater eel is an unusual fish   _____

2. People often see these fish in lakes and rivers   _____

3. But never saw a young, baby eel   _____

4. Did not know where the eel was born   _____

5. The life of the eel is truly amazing   _____

6. Long journeys at the beginning and at the end of its life   _____

7. Swims down rivers of Europe and North America   _____

8. The eel then goes for many miles across the ocean   _____

9. Journey about six months long   _____

10. Here in the western Atlantic the journey ends   _____

II. Place the correct punctuation mark at the end of each sentence below.

11. The eggs of the eel are hatched in the Atlantic Ocean
12. What happens then to the larvae
13. The Gulf Stream carries them to shallow waters
14. What a long journey they must make
15. After about two and a half years, the journey ends
16. Do the larvae now change to eels
17. But what an unusual appearance the young fish have
18. The name ''glass eels'' is given to young, transparent eels
19. Is their journey over when they reach the shores
20. The male eels remain near the shore of the ocean
21. The females find their way up the mouths of rivers
22. How far they sometimes travel
23. Do eels grow to full size in freshwater
24. At last the fish return down the rivers to the Atlantic Ocean
25. Don't they make the long journey back to their birthplace
26. Here, where they were born, the eels lay their eggs before they die

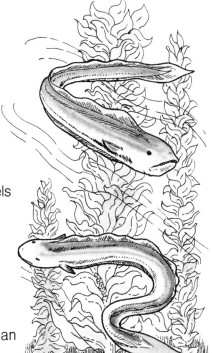

Reviewing Subject and Predicate   ⚷ 45

I. In each sentence draw a line under the complete subject. Write each simple subject on the line at the right of the sentence. (Score: 23—1 for each complete subject and 1 for each simple subject)

The Saint Bernard

1.   The Alps lie between Italy and Switzerland.   _____

2.   Several roads lead from one country to another.   _____

3.   These roads must pass over the towering mountains.   _____

4.   Terrible snowstorms often rage in the mountain passes.   _____

5.   Travelers of long ago were often caught in storms.   _____

6.   The travelers sometimes lost their way.   _____

7.   A monastery was established in this region.   _____

8.   The purpose of the monastery was to help travelers.   _____

9.   Men from the monastery searched for lost travelers.   _____

10.   Huge dogs, called Saint Bernards, helped in the search.   _____

11.   The men and the dogs saved many lives.   _____

II. Draw a line under the complete predicate. Write each simple predicate on the line at the right. (Score: 19—1 for each complete predicate and 1 for each simple predicate)

12.   Lost people were sometimes buried in the snow.   _____

13.   The searchers might have missed them.   _____

14.   But the keen-scented dogs would usually find them.   _____

15.   In snowstorms people lose their sense of direction.   _____

16.   They were not always able to return.   _____

17.   Then the Saint Bernards are especially valuable.   _____

18.   They can safely lead the way through the storm.   _____

19.   They apparently sense the approach of a stranger.   _____

20.   The barking dogs are released from the monastery.   _____

21.   The dogs find the stranger and return for help.   _____

Reviewing Nouns and Pronouns   ⛏ 13–20

I.   Write the plural forms of the nouns listed below. (Score: 8)

1.   concerto _____   5.   shelf   _____

2.   match   _____   6.   penny   _____

3.   knife   _____   7.   woman   _____

4.   potato   _____   8.   goose   _____

II.   Write the possessive forms of the following words. (Score: 4)

9.   men   _____   11.   ponies   _____

10.   Bess   _____   12.   candy   _____

III.   Draw one line under each noun and two lines under each pronoun in the following sentences. (Score: 17)

13.   Many people dreamed of building the Panama Canal.

14.   France was the first country that tried to build it.

15.   But the French were stopped by the tiny mosquito.

16.   The insect gave them the terrible yellow fever.

17.   Perhaps you have heard of Walter Reed, the scientist.

18.   He was the man who finally conquered the deadly fever.

IV.   Underline the proper pronoun in parentheses. (Score: 7)

19.   Ellen told Bob and (I, me) that France gave up its attempt to build the canal.

20.   (He, Him) and (I, me) knew that the United States bought the land.

21.   Ellen told (we, us) that work began three years later.

22.   It was (I, me) who knew what was done first.

23.   (Us, We) knew that the mosquitoes were destroyed.

24.   It was (she, her) who said that this work took three years.

V.   In the blank at the right of the following sentences write the proper pronoun to take the place of the noun or word group in italics. (Score: 4)

25.   *Karen* said that work began on the canal in 1906.   _____

26.   *Bob and Ellen* asked when it was finished.   _____

27.   Karen told *Bob and Ellen* that the canal was finished in 1914.   _____

28.   The first ship passed through *the canal* in August, 1914.   _____

Reviewing Verbs

O━ 21, 22, 24

I. Fill in the missing principal parts of the verbs below. (Score: 20)

1. _____ swim _____   _____   _____

2. _____   _____   _____ lain _____

3. _____   _____ broke _____   _____

4. _____   _____   _____ eaten _____

5. _____ lay _____   _____   _____

6. _____   _____ knew _____   _____

7. _____   _____   _____ written _____

8. _____ bring _____   _____   _____

9. _____   _____ saw _____   _____

10. _____ choose _____   _____   _____

II. Draw a line under the verb or verb phrase in each sentence below.

11.   Perhaps you have seen meteors in the sky.

12.   Meteors are sometimes called "shooting stars."

13.   But meteors are not stars at all.

14.   They are composed of dust or rock.

15.   Perhaps the meteor has flown through space for centuries.

16.   Then it has fallen toward Earth.

17.   Suddenly the meteor has burst into a bright light.

18.   This light was caused by friction.

19.   The meteor moves at very great speeds.

20.   The speed has been estimated at 82 kilometers (50 miles) per second.

21.   Then the meteor has entered the earth's atmosphere.

22.   There is friction between the meteor and the atmosphere.

23.   A tremendous heat is caused by this friction.

24.   The meteor's light is produced by the heat.

25.   Most meteors are burned away by this heat.

26.   But meteors have sometimes been found on Earth.

27.   The meteor may have once been part of a comet.

Reviewing Adjectives and Adverbs   ⌐ 25, 26

I. Draw one line under the adjective in each sentence below. On the line at the right of the sentence write the word that is modified by the adjective. Do not underline the articles *a, an,* or *the*.

The Story of Pompeii

1.   In Italy there is a famous volcano called Vesuvius.   _____

2.   The volcano has often caused great damage.   _____

3.   A Roman city stood near Vesuvius centuries ago.   _____

4.   This beautiful city was named Pompeii.   _____

5.   Many Romans built their homes in Pompeii.   _____

6.   The mighty Vesuvius erupted in the year 79.   _____

7.   The eruptions continued for two days.   _____

8.   The city was buried under a thick layer of ashes.   _____

II.   Draw a line under the adverb in each sentence below. On the line at the right of the sentence write the word or words that are modified by the adverb.

9.   As years passed, people almost forgot Pompeii.   _____

10.   Trees slowly grew on the ashes from the volcano.   _____

11.   The ashes made an extremely rich soil.   _____

12.   Farmers successfully grew crops over the buried city.   _____

13.   Nobody ever thought of the ancient Pompeii.   _____

14.   But people finally dug through the deep ashes.   _____

15.   They were greatly amazed when they found Pompeii.   _____

16.   Beautifully decorated homes and temples were found.   _____

17.   The ruins added immensely to our knowledge of Rome.   _____

18.   Highly skilled workers restored these ruins.   _____

19.   In 1980 an earthquake seriously damaged parts of Italy.   _____

20.   Some ruins were severely cracked in the quake.   _____

21.   Again, workers restore the ancient city of Pompeii.   _____

Reviewing Prepositions   ⚷ 27

Leonardo da Vinci

I. Draw a line under each preposition in the sentences below. (Score: 10)

1. Leonardo da Vinci was one of the world's most amazing people.
2. This fifteenth-century Italian artist is famous for his beautiful paintings.
3. The *Mona Lisa* portrait is known throughout the world.
4. *The Last Supper* is also among the world's most famous paintings.
5. Many beautiful statues were made by this man, too.
6. He was the architect of many beautiful buildings.
7. Leonardo went to Milan, Italy, when he was a young man.
8. He designed several canals in this city.
9. Canal boats could then travel through the city.
10. Today, after five centuries, the canals are still being used.

II. Underline the prepositional phrase in each sentence below. On the line at the right tell whether the phrase is used as an adjective or as an adverb. Use the abbreviations *adj.* and *adv.* (Score: 14)

11. Leonardo was also interested in science.   _____

12. He drew plans for a flying machine.   _____

13. It was a board with movable wings.   _____

14. The machine would fly like a bird.   _____

15. A person would lie on the board.   _____

16. The wings would be moved by a person's feet.   _____

17. But Leonardo's design for an "airplane" was not used. _____

III. Underline the proper preposition in parentheses. (Score: 8)

18. Leonardo often received gifts of money (off of, from) the King of France.
19. Once Leonardo built a large model (off, of) a lion for this King.
20. The lion was brought (into, in) the King's throne room.
21. Everyone (in, into) the room was amazed when the lion "roared."
22. Other mechanical toys were (between, among) Leonardo's many inventions.
23. Sometimes he picked up rocks (off, off of) the ground.
24. Then he would study the differences (between, among) two rocks.
25. The weather was another (of, off) the many subjects Leonardo studied.

Reviewing Conjunctions and Interjections   ⚷ 28, 29

I. Combine the following pairs of sentences, using one of the conjunctions listed below. Do not use any one conjunction more than two times. You may make slight changes in the wording of the sentences. (Score: 3 for each sentence)

Example: We shall go. The day is warm. *We shall go because the day is warm.*

although	and	for	as	while
because	but	if	when	until

Dirigibles

1. Once dirigibles were fairly common. Today they are seldom seen. _____

_____

2. Airplanes were still clumsy. People began to build dirigibles. _____

_____

3. The dirigibles were beautiful. They were dangerous! _____

_____

4. The dirigibles used hydrogen. Hydrogen is a lightweight gas. _____

_____

5. The dirigible was filled with hydrogen. The dirigible floated. _____

_____

6. Hydrogen weighs less than air. It could lift the dirigible. _____

_____

7. What a dangerous gas it was! It exploded easily. _____

_____

8. How amazed people were! A dirigible crossed the Atlantic in four days. _____

_____

9. Airplanes were improved. Fewer dirigibles were built. _____

_____

II.   List three interjections on the lines below. (Score: 3)

10. _____   11. _____   12. _____

Reviewing Capitalization and Punctuation   ⚮ 1–11

Draw a line under each letter that should be capitalized. Place punctuation marks where they are needed.

Margaret Mead

1. Have you read about margaret Mead, the anthropologist
2. She is known for her studies of people in other societies
3. In 1925 she made her first field trip to the South seas
4. She observed the children on the island of tau in samoa.
5. She studied the primitive culture on this island
6. dr Mead wrote a book about what she learned
7. How popular her book became
8. Did she make another trip in 1928
9. Yes she went to the admiralty islands
10. She went on several trips to new guinea during her lifetime
11. Wasn't dr Mead born on december 16 1901
12. Yes and she grew up in philadelphia pennsylvania
13. How far away her studies took her
14. I would like to travel like dr. Mead said Steven
15. She taught at columbia university in new york
16. Did she also work at the american museum of natural history
17. My aunt pam has read the book, blackberry winter.
18. Margaret Mead wrote this book about her life said Lisa
19. ''Dr Mead also worked for the u s government '' Steven added.
20. During world war ll she wrote booklets to aid american and british troops.
21. My aunt said that dr Mead lived for many years in new york said Lisa.
22. She once heard her speak there
23. Did she give many speeches about her travels asked Steven.
24. Yes she continued to speak and write throughout her life answered Lisa.
25. Do you think she took many pictures during her travels asked Steven.
26. I would like to see pictures of the islands
27. While studying the peoples of bali, she took many pictures answered Lisa
28. What a fascinating book these pictures made
29. Scientists in europe and the united states praised her work.
30. She was one of the first people to make complete studies of other cultures
31. Margaret Mead died in new york on november 15 1978.
32. She made a great contribution to the social sciences

Reviewing Proper Forms

17, 20, 25–27, 34–36, 40

Draw a line under the proper expression in parentheses.

Unusual Desert Plants

1. Deserts are places where scarcely (any, no) kind of plants can grow.

2. There is not (no, any) moisture to speak of in such regions.

3. Shifting desert sand makes it (real, very) hard for plants to establish roots.

4. Hot, bare rocks make it difficult for plants to gain a foothold, (to, too, two).

5. In spite of the formidable conditions, some plants grow (good, well) in deserts.

6. The cactus plant is well suited to (its, it's) life in the desert.

7. Leaves of most plants allow water (to, too, two) evaporate into the air.

8. Cacti (have, have got) very few, if any, leaves.

9. They hold (their, there) water (in, into) their thick, fleshy stems.

10. Cacti make food for (themselves, theirselves) in their stems.

11. Roots of (them, those) plants grow near the top of the ground.

12. They spread out over a (wide, widely) area to catch as much water as possible.

13. These plants are (covered, covered over) with many sharp spines.

14. The spines have kept away many animals that (might of, might have) eaten the plants.

15. Many different sizes and shapes are found (between, among) the various cactus plants.

16. Some cacti are (not never, never) very big, but others grow as large as trees.

17. A forest of giant cacti is a strange sight to (sea, see).

18. Many of these plants grow fifty feet high and have (no, know) fewer than fifty arms.

19. Fruits taken (off, off of) these plants are often used to make cactus preserves.

20. The state of Arizona chose the giant cactus for (its, it's) state flower.

21. The "barrel cactus" looks somewhat like (a, an) upside-down nail keg.

22. (This, This here) cactus is round and grows close to the ground.

23. Many desert travelers (no, know) that the juice in a barrel cactus is good to drink.

24. One kind of cactus has white flowers that are (not hardly, hardly) ever seen.

25. Maria told Helen and (I, me) that the night-blooming cereus opens only at night.

26. The person (who, which) developed a spineless cactus was Luther Burbank.

27. (We, Us) want to make a garden with many different varieties of cacti.

28. The boys said that it was (they, them) (who, which) gave us the idea for a garden.

29. Ben and (I, me) gave (a, an) "moon cactus" to Judy and (she, her).

30. Tom and (they, them) said that cacti (hadn't ought, ought not) to be watered much.

31. Helen said that cacti grow (real, very) slowly.

32. We are all eager to (see, sea) the planted garden.

Remembering What We Have Learned

1. On the lines below write one declarative, one interrogative, and one exclamatory sentence. 🔑 44

_____

_____

_____

2. Rewrite the following sentences, using capital letters and punctuation marks where they are needed. 🔑 1-11

on saturday march 21 2007 sam went to washington d c _____

_____

oh! how exciting it was to see the white house _____

_____

he saw the senate in session at the u s capitol _____

_____

ms smith i would like to be a senator said sam _____

_____

dont senators play an important role in our government _____

_____

3. On each line below write a word from the sentences above to illustrate the part of speech indicated at the left of the line. 🔑 13-29

noun   _____   adverb   _____

pronoun   _____   preposition   _____

verb   _____   conjunction   _____

adjective   _____   interjection _____

4. On the lines below write the three principal parts of a verb. 🔑 24

_____   _____   _____

5.   On the first line below write the singular and plural forms of two nouns. On the second line write the possessive forms of the four words.   🔑 14, 15

_____   _____   _____   _____

_____   _____   _____   _____

6.   Write a sentence in which you use a prepositional phrase as an adjective.   🔑 27

_____

7.   Write a pair of synonyms in the first two blanks and a pair of homophones in the last two blanks.   🔑 38, 40

_____   _____   _____   _____

8.   Write three three-syllable words in alphabetical order. Put hyphens between the syllables, and place an accent mark after the accented syllable of each word.   🔑 41, 42

_____   _____   _____

9.   On each line write a sentence, using one of the words or groups of words in parentheses at the left of the line.   🔑 17, 20, 23–27, 40

(between, among) _____

(in, into) _____

(good, well) _____

(quick, quickly) _____

(himself, themselves) _____

(who, which) _____

(grew, grown) _____

(saw, seen) _____

(broke, broken) _____

(play, plays) _____

(is, are) _____

(she and I, her and me) _____

(we, us) _____

(your, you're) _____

(their, there) _____

Index of Lessons

NOTE: Numbers after the entries refer to page numbers. Only pages on which the subject is emphasized are listed.

Index of Informational Topics and Stories in Lessons

NOTE: Numbers following the entries are page numbers.

Index of The Text

NOTE: Numbers following the entries refer to key numbers, not to page numbers.